Little Laureates

Poets From Suffolk

Edited by Claire Tupholme

YoungWriters

First published in Great Britain in 2008 by:
Young Writers
Remus House
Coltsfoot Drive
Peterborough
PE2 9JX
Telephone: 01733 890066
Website: www.youngwriters.co.uk

SB ISBN 978-1 84431 491 1

Foreword

Young Writers was established in 1991 and has been passionately devoted to the promotion of reading and writing in children and young adults ever since. The quest continues today. Young Writers remains as committed to the nurturing of poetic and literary talent as ever.

This year's Young Writers competition has proven as vibrant and dynamic as ever and we are delighted to present a showcase of the best poetry from across the UK and in some cases overseas. Each poem has been selected from a wealth of *Little Laureates* entries before ultimately being published in this, our sixteenth primary school poetry series.

Once again, we have been supremely impressed by the overall quality of the entries we have received. The imagination, energy and creativity which has gone into each young writer's entry made choosing the poems a challenging and often difficult but ultimately hugely rewarding task - the general high standard of the work submitted ensured this opportunity to bring their poetry to a larger appreciative audience.

We sincerely hope you are pleased with this final collection and that you will enjoy *Little Laureates Poets From Suffolk* for many years to come.

Contents

The Poems

Love

Love is a big slice of ham and pineapple pizza.
Love is being able to dress up in big floaty dresses.
Love is a softly-flowing river of hearts.
Love is a beautiful bunch of red roses.
Love is the soft sound of my cat Binka purring away to me.
Love is someone reaching out to help you.
Love is someone special.
Love is a big box of chocolates.
Love is a feeling nothing can replace.

Olivia Palmer (9)

The Planets

Mercury whizzing around and around the sun like lightning.
Venus raining acid from big, thick, yellow clouds.
Earth rolling and crashing like a big beach ball.
Mars is called the Red Planet because the rocks and soil are
a reddish-brown colour.
Jupiter is the largest planet made of lumps of rock called asteroids.
Saturn has many more planets than any other planet.
Uranus is a blue and green big, big ball.
Neptune has a dark ring around it and it is a blue colour.
Pluto is the smallest in our solar system.

Abbie Colegate (9)
Acton CE (VC) Primary School

The Planets

Mercury spinning and twisting and turning and moving around the sun.
Venus raining acid from thick yellow clouds.
Earth, life is on Earth, water and food for the humans.
Mars, the fourth planet, the first and largest of the giant planets.
Saturn's rings are made of ice and rock.

Millie Walton (8)
Acton CE (VC) Primary School

Amy's Wonderful Pets

In my bedroom I kept . . .
Ten dazzling dolphins diving in the pool,
Nine old octopuses sliming up the wall,
Eight enormous elephants making silly noises everywhere,
Seven slimy snakes slithering along my bed,
Six messy monkeys fighting over Ted,
Five jumpy jaguars playing draughts with the elephants,
Four fluffy polar bears cuddling me tight,
Three lonely lions waiting for some company,
Two funny frogs hopping up and down
And one guess what? Me!

Amy Sawyer (8)
Acton CE (VC) Primary School

Ronan's Crazy Pets

In my bedroom I kept . . .
Ten laughing hyenas doing lots of jumping everywhere
Nine swinging monkeys hanging from the light,
Eight elephants stomping around in clogs,
Seven rhinos charging at the monkeys,
Six crocodiles crunching my toys,
Five slithery snakes sliding over my bed,
Four falcons swooping over my head,
Three water hogs snoozing in my bed,
Two tired tigers trying to get to sleep
And one guess what? Me!

Ronan Beckett (8)
Acton CE (VC) Primary School

Madeline's Mad House

In my bedroom I kept . . .
Ten thumping serpents thumping on the floor, you're going to break the floor!
Nine attacking alligators under my bed,
Eight cheeky monkeys bouncing on my bed,
Seven baby tigers shouting down the phone, that's loud!
Six charging rhinos trying to break down the floor,
Five squawking parrots flapping feathers everywhere,
Four digging moles making holes in my carpet,
Three huge elephants rolling in the mud,
Two spotty leopards lazing on the wardrobe,
One guess who? Me!

Madeline Starkey (8)
Acton CE (VC) Primary School

Liam's Zuper Zoo

In my bedroom I kept . . .
Ten bouncing kangaroos jumping on my bed,
Nine tough gorillas smashing my window,
Eight fast chinchillas watching TV,
Seven massive elephants dancing two by two,
Six snapping crocodiles crawling under my bed,
Five curling orang-utans swinging on my light,
Four leaping dolphins glistening on the floor,
Three spring tigers scratching on the wall, that's gotta hurt the ladies' nails!
Two charging rhinos banging on the wardrobe
And one guess what? Me!

Liam Mortin (8)
Acton CE (VC) Primary School

Anna's Crazy Pets

In my bedroom I kept . . .
Ten snapping crocodiles growling in my wardrobe,
Nine cheeky monkeys hanging out the window,
Eight paddling polar bears stomping up the wall,
Seven weird pandas playing on the phone, don't waste the battery!
Six squawking parrots playing on the PlayStation,
Five laughing hyenas scratching on the wall, oh no, not the wall!
Four spiky hedgehogs rolling around,
Three slimy snakes hissing at my dad,
Two fluffy rabbits nibbling on my slippers
And one guess what? Me!

Anna Holmes (8)
Acton CE (VC) Primary School

Sam's Circus

In my bedroom I kept . . .
Ten terrific cows mooing at the window,
Nine weird hedgehogs playing on the PlayStation,
Eight gulping fish gulping in their bowl,
Seven greedy mice nibbling bread and cheese, don't leave them
crumbs on my bed!
Six angry bears trying to eat the cows,
Five classic cats doing a pose,
Four silent doves gazing at the TV,
Three fantastic owls singing, *tweet-tweet*
Two leaping rabbits pouncing around on the ground
And one guess what? Me!

Sam Phillips (8)
Acton CE (VC) Primary School

Danny's Mad Pets

In my bedroom I kept . . .
Ten fiery dragons eating my roof,
Nine hungry caterpillars munching at my pictures,
Eight spooky bats flying over my mum's head, go away!
Seven cheeky monkeys swinging corner to corner,
Six cats jumping up my wall,
Five fish leaping out my window,
Four polar bears on my PlayStation 2,
Three laughing cheetahs jumping on my bed,
Two brave kangaroos watching TV
And one guess what? Me!

Danny Emerton (8)
Acton CE (VC) Primary School

Jordan's Pets

In my bedroom I kept . . .
Ten terrific tigers tramping towards me,
Nine naughty monkeys swinging from corner to corner,
Eight elephants thumping round my bed,
Seven slithering snakes under my wardrobe,
Six little squirrels cracking nuts which make a noise,
Five funny fish swimming in their tank,
Four crazy chickens pecking at me,
Three thirsty gerbils looking for a drink,
Two dogs fighting over a bone
And one guess what? Me!

Jordan Sargeant (9)
Acton CE (VC) Primary School

Chloe's Crazy Pets

In my bedroom I kept . . .
Ten messy monkeys hanging on the light,
Nine munching chinchillas chomping all my books,
Eight dancing polar bears spinning to YMCA,
Seven sparkling ponies galloping around the room,
Six scorpions stinging me, *ouch!*
Five leaping kangaroos bouncing on my bed,
Four silky dolphins hiding in the wardrobe,
Three spiky hedgehogs crunching my carpet,
Two noisy elephants making a terrific bang with their feet
And one guess what? Me!

Chloe Miles (8)
Acton CE (VC) Primary School

Joe's Fantastic Pets

In my bedroom I kept . . .
Ten terrible tigers gobbling all my sweets,
Nine nasty monkeys playing on my PS2,
Eight enormous rhinos charging at my mum, help!
Seven wide hippos squashing my favourite toys,
Six slithery snakes licking all my teddies,
Five lazy lions tracking down my brother, run for it!
Four mad gorillas smashing the cups,
Three fluffy polar bears snoozing on my bed,
Two dumb elephants jumping on my bed
And one guess what? Me!

Joe Moye (8)
Acton CE (VC) Primary School

Phyllis' Unusual Pets

In my bedroom I kept . . .
Ten roaring tigers crawling under my bed,
Nine naughty monkeys jumping on my head, stop that!
Eight stomping elephants dancing on the chair,
Seven slimy snakes wriggling everywhere,
Six racing snails hiding behind the bed,
Five tiny whales opening the window,
Four quacking ducks swimming in my bowl of soup,
Three noisy dogs staring at the mirror,
Two flying frogs pretending I'm a tree
And one guess what? Me!

Phyllis Ruse (8)
Acton CE (VC) Primary School

Rocket Poem

R ockets shoot up into space
O ut jumps a firework and then it goes *bang!*
C an you spot them going up and down?
K itten is scared near the bonfire
E ating my dinner outside
T he toilet is blocked so I cannot go!

Chiara Jenkins & Megan Manfield (7)
Badwell Ash CE (VA) Primary School

Autumn Time

Leaves turn colours
Red, yellow, brown
See them fall off the branches
Floating down.

Jordan Pratt (7)
Badwell Ash CE (VA) Primary School

Autumn Poem

A ll the leaves falling from trees
U nder the leaves little bugs open
T he little bugs crawl away
U nder bushes insects live
M agnificent brown and orange leaves fall
N ew grass growing on lands

I t's new
S ummer will come again

B rown leaves fall to the ground
R ound the land leaves fall
I will play in the leaves
L eaves love to play in the air
L ovely wind blows past
I t's great
A nice lovely day
N ice clouds race away
T oday is very nice in autumn.

Matthew Kennedy (8)
Badwell Ash CE (VA) Primary School

The Autumn Poem

L ovely autumn
O f beautiful leaves
V elvet catkins
E verything is colourful
L emon colours and orange
Y ellowy leaves falling from the trees

A utumn leaves all beautiful colours
U p above the treetops the clouds race
T rees lose their leaves
U nder the leaves the bugs crawl
M y friend and I gather the leaves
N eeding some help from Mum and Dad.

Amy Bird (9)
Badwell Ash CE (VA) Primary School

Autumn Poems

A ll the leaves fall
U nder the trees
T he little bugs crawl
U p above, the clouds turn grey
M y heart is full of joy
N ow leaves come again

I t is true
S unny days will come again

B ursting out with joy
R acing, racing through the sky
I will win in the sky
L eaves covering the air
L iving in the trees now on the ground
I sn't it great
A lovely day
N ice isn't it
T he autumn.

Ethan Bartholomew (8)
Badwell Ash CE (VA) Primary School

Autumn Poem

A ll of the leaves float to the ground
U nder the leaves
T he small bugs crawl
U p above the wind blows
M y tree house is full of leaves
N earby children play in all the piles of leaves

I t is the time for me to
S weep up all the leaves

F lowers dying every minute
U sing leaves to jump in
N ow it is time for winter.

Jordan Sylvester (9)
Badwell Ash CE (VA) Primary School

The Witches' Spell

(Based on 'Macbeth')

'Double, double, toil and trouble
Fire burn and cauldron bubble'

Toe of toad, tiny terrapin tickle
Nose of a newt, a little bit of pickle.
Leg of a lion, wing of bat,
Eye of pig and a pointy hat.
Heart of horse, mix it up.

'Double, double, toil and trouble,
Fire burn and cauldron bubble'

Alec Lawson (7)
Badwell Ash CE (VA) Primary School

Autumn

A utumn leaves start to fall
U nder the leaves the little bugs crawl
T he beautiful leaves fall
U sing leaves are fun
M y garden is full with leaves
N othing is more fun then autumn.

Sophie Cobbold (9)
Badwell Ash CE (VA) Primary School

Autumn

A utumn is a fun time of year
U nder the trees are some colourful leaves
T he leaves are fun
U sing leaves is so much fun
M y garden is full of leaves
N eighbours are overrun with leaves.

James Starie (7)
Badwell Ash CE (VA) Primary School

Witches' Spell

(Based on 'Macbeth')

'Double, double, toil and trouble,
Fire burn and cauldron bubble'

A jaguar's claw and a tiger's tongue,
A fox's fur and a vine snake swung.
A tarantula's bite and scorpion's sting,
A fish's fin and a whale's swing.
Elephant's tail all eaten by a snail,
Cat with a flea and a snake up in a tree.

'Double, double, toil and trouble,
Fire burn and cauldron bubble'

Sam Bassett (8)
Badwell Ash CE (VA) Primary School

Autumn Colours

Brown leaves float
Red foxes run
Yellow leaves lying
Green grass grows
Blackberry bushes
Hidden rabbits.

Ben Bassett (7)
Badwell Ash CE (VA) Primary School

Autumn

The trees are growing,
The leaves are falling
Pretty colours are around.
The leaves are changing colour to red and yellow.

Callum Sharpe (7)
Badwell Ash CE (VA) Primary School

The Witches' Spell

(Based on 'Macbeth')

'Double, double, toil and trouble,
Fire burn and cauldron bubble'

Leg of a rat and horse's hoof,
Rabbit tail and a tortoise roof.
Cat's eye and a slithering snake,
Fly's wing and a point of a rake.
Lion's fur and a golden dog's ear,
Cheetah's spots and a pint of beer.
A bat's tooth and a giant's hair,
A fish's fin and a nose of a bear.

'Double, double, toil and trouble,
Fire burn and cauldron bubble'

Samantha Smith (8)
Badwell Ash CE (VA) Primary School

The Spear Of Freedom

I am a soldier, I'm strong and I'm keen,
I fight for my country, I don't care if I'm mean.
The knights are coming, they're coming here,
And as I heard this I grabbed my spear.
We started to fight with all our might,
There were a hundred in the night
I only killed one knight.
But in the middle of the fight,
I spotted a king,
His name was Ling.
We jumped apart,
I speared him through the heart.
The knights had gone and I was free
But one day I knew they'd come back to get 'em!

Sam Chapman (8)
Badwell Ash CE (VA) Primary School

My Nightmare

One night long ago
I was in a forest full of monsters.
I walked forward,
My feet were stuck in mud.
I saw two shadows
So I said, 'Go away.'
There was a plane in the sky
It was a bad plane
So we ran and ran.
We lost it at last
Then we killed the monsters
And I was back in my bed.

Sara Johnson (8)
Badwell Ash CE (VA) Primary School

Hate

Hate is the colour of black darkness.
Hate sounds like roaring thunder.
Hate tastes like five strong chillies.
Hate smells like an erupting volcano.
Hate looks like fire burning.
Hate feels like hot water.
Hate reminds me of the Devil.

Jack Cresswell (9)
Castle Hill Junior School

Anger

Anger is red like chillies I've been fed.
Anger sounds like steaming volcanoes.
Anger smells like an empty nothing at all that makes me look
like a big fool.
Anger feels bad like I want to kill *you!*

Ethan Flack (9)
Castle Hill Junior School

Hate

The colour of hate is dark red like an exploding volcano.
The sound of hate is like a grizzly bear attacking something.
The taste of hate is hot like a spicy chilli that's about to burst
in your mouth.
The smell of hate smells of a burning fire that is flaming
around everywhere.
The look of hate is like you're just about to get punched in your face
and you're about to be knocked out.
The feel of hate is like you're sticking your face in a bowl
of scorching hot water.
Hate reminds me of when I got really annoyed with my brother
and when my face went bright red.

Haydn Chaplin (10)
Castle Hill Junior School

Love

Love is the colour of a bright pink fuchsia opening.
Love sounds like bells rattling making a lovely noise.
Love smells like a pretty rose opening.
Love looks like a heart opening upon my head.
Love feels like the person inside me I can trust.
Love reminds me of a special wedding day.

Georgia Laughlin (9)
Castle Hill Junior School

Silence

Silence is like a mouse crawling along the floor.
Silence is nothing, nothing at all.
Silence feels like sand slipping through your hands
on a cold misty beach.
Silence reminds me of when I am alone.
Silence is a dark misty day.

Nadia Jolly (9)
Castle Hill Junior School

Anger

Anger is like an angry hungry bear exploding.
Anger sounds like a pounding volcano bellowing in your brain.
It tastes like fire burning on your tongue, red, orange, yellow.
Anger smells of a bonfire after it's been lit.
Anger looks like a blaze of raging fire.
Anger feels like someone putting dynamite inside you.
Anger reminds me of a fire-breathing dragon after birth
and the roaring of its mum.

Kelsea Gooding (9)
Castle Hill Junior School

Happiness

Happiness is the colours of the rainbow like a wish is coming true.
Happiness sounds like a breeze washing towards me slowly.
Happiness tastes like a piece of chocolate melting in your mouth.
Happiness smells like perfume coming off flowers floating calmly.
Happiness looks like the moon glittering in the sky.
Happiness feels like a boat floating down the river at night
and hotels lighting up.
Happiness reminds me of a rainbow sparkling in the air.

Tia Horman (9)
Castle Hill Junior School

Love

Love is pink like falling into a land of pillows.
Love sounds like someone dancing to music that's sweet.
Love tastes like oozing chocolate fountains falling onto friendly willows.
Love looks like couples kissing on a deserted beach.
Love smells like beautiful summer roses burning in the hot heat.
Love feels like you're falling into lovely arms and never getting hurt.
Love reminds me of drowning in a puddle and always getting
pulled out.

Courtney Smith (9)
Castle Hill Junior School

Sadness

Sadness is a blueberry going rotten.
Sadness sounds like someone sweeping faintly in a dark graveyard.
Sadness tastes like a piece of steaming hot chilli.
Sadness smells like the stinky smell of the water under the sea.
Sadness feels like people have left you to sit down in heavy rain
and clashing thunder.
Sadness looks like someone has been horrible by starving you
and hurting you.
Sadness reminds me that there are times when people leave me out
and make me sit on my own.

Devon Draper (9)
Castle Hill Junior School

Love

The colour of love is pink sweet-smelling roses.
The sound of love is little blue tits singing in my ears.
The taste of love is creamy chocolate oozing with caramel.
The smell of love is beautiful poppies swaying side to side.
Love looks like a happy couple kissing on their wedding day.
Love feels like a big breath of fresh air.
Love reminds me of a happy wedding.

Chelsea Sparrow (9)
Castle Hill Junior School

When I Am Happy

When I am happy I think of light blue like the sunny sky.
When I am happy I think of singing birds in my head.
When I am happy I think of the taste of apple pie.
When I am happy I think of the scent of flowers.
When I am happy I think of little tiny bunnies.
When I am happy I think of being in a meadow of flowers.
When I am happy I think of my family.

Emily Delany (9)
Castle Hill Junior School

Darkness

Darkness is black like spilt petrol.
Darkness sounds like a dying man in the forest.
Darkness tastes like drinking spilt oil off the ground.
Darkness smells like people drowning in the ocean.
Darkness looks like a little dog in a haunted house.
Darkness feels like a slimy hand on my neck.
Darkness reminds me of me in the cemetery and zombies jumping,
With a single hand on my shoulder, I said, *'Argh!'*

Owen Hughes (9)
Castle Hill Junior School

Darkness

The colour of darkness is gloomy monster black.
The sound of darkness is the shimmery owls talking.
The taste of darkness is the burning liquorice sliding into your mouth.
The smell of darkness is like a cold scary evening.
The look of darkness is like a person standing on their own
in a school playground.
The feel of darkness is like a cold wind blowing in my face.
Darkness reminds me of a cold Christmas Eve.

Emily Fletcher (9)
Castle Hill Junior School

Darkness

Darkness is black like newly spilt oil.
Darkness sounds like distant drums.
Darkness tastes like nothing at all and sprouts.
Darkness smells like rotting bones.
Darkness looks like misty days and gloomy stones.
Darkness feels scary, frightening and freaky when someone shouts.
Darkness reminds me of a gloomy graveyard
And then the zombies and ghouls come out and shout, *'Boo!'*

Nic Hedges (9)
Castle Hill Junior School

Anger

Anger is like red-hot lava crashing through the rocks.
Anger sounds like lightning and thunder dashing through the sky.
Anger tastes like flaming red-hot chilli.
Anger smells like your beans are burning and you're on fire.
Anger looks like a fierce lion jumping out at you.
Anger is when you're getting so annoyed you just want
to smash something.
Anger reminds me there's an earthquake in your head
and you just can't stop your anger.

Ilda Duka (9)
Castle Hill Junior School

Fear!

The colour of fear is like the darkness of the midnight sky.
The sound of fear is like a loud shot or cry.
The taste of fear is like hot chillies burnt today.
The smell of fear is like an old abandoned motorway.
Fear looks like someone rotten in the middle of the road.
It feels like the raging fire of the midnight sun.
It reminds me of being lifted off your feet in a dark room.

Alexander Moore (10)
Castle Hill Junior School

Hunger

Hunger is like white in your stomach.
Hunger is the sound of bubbling drinks but tastes rather disgusting.
Hunger is a smell like hot chilli with feet.
Hunger looks all gooey like some ghost bogeys.
Hunger feels like some hairy monsters.
Hunger reminds me of when my team are losing.

Thomas Peters (9)
Castle Hill Junior School

Darkness

Darkness is grey like a November day.
Darkness sounds like battering drums.
Darkness tastes like a stale out of date crisp.
Darkness smells like a lurking fog and a graveyard mist.
Darkness looks like a cinema with a flickering screen.
Darkness feels so empty and mean
And when I remember I feel so glad that we're in the light
And we don't feel the night fright!

Tyler Berry (9)
Castle Hill Junior School

Fear

Fear is grey like a hungry, scavenger wolf
Fear sounds like a bellowing hunger-driven bear.
Fear tastes like a bitter soggy sandwich.
Fear smells like a foggy, misty day.
Fear looks like a weak dog begging for food.
Fear feels like a cold wind pushing against the graveyard grass.
Fear reminds me of a knight facing his fears.

Nicola Beckett (9)
Castle Hill Junior School

Love

The colour of love is the colour of a gliding white swan.
The sound of love is a violin playing soft music.
The taste of love is pink and blue candyfloss.
The smell of love is the soft-scented perfume.
The look of love is a giant red love heart right in front of your eyes.
Love feels like fluffy, white, cotton clouds.
Love reminds me of me and my family.

Melissa Gurner (9)
Castle Hill Junior School

Darkness

Darkness is black and as cold as a razor blade that has never
been made.
Darkness sounds like the drip from a wall and a whale's call.
Darkness tastes like yucky Kentucky.
Darkness smells like a damp, wet cave.
Darkness looks like a man who needs a shave
Darkness feels so wet and cold I wish I did what I was told.
Darkness reminds me of a dark room so dark and gloomy.

Ellie Boreham (9)
Castle Hill Junior School

Happiness

Happiness is the colours of the rainbow that spreads in the sky.
Happiness sounds like clowns laughing until their trousers split.
Happiness tastes like sweets that never lie.
Happiness smells like lavender, I hope I'm not being too mad.
Happiness looks like trees swaying in the sun.
Happiness feels like soft, wet grass.
Happiness reminds me of a gorgeous chocolate bun, yum!

Amy Backhouse (9)
Castle Hill Junior School

Hunger

The colour of hunger is white.
The sound of hunger is a rumble.
The taste of hunger is nothing.
The smell smells like an empty stomach.
The look is see-through.
The feel of hunger is like a digestive system.
Hunger reminds me of my team losing.

Scott Bartlett (9)
Castle Hill Junior School

My Magic Wellie Boots

One day I went outside to play, it was raining cats and dogs,
Good weather for fish or sealife and maybe even frogs!

So I had to get back in the house as fast as I could run,
And sensibly put my wellie boots on, carefully, one by one.

I ran back into the garden to have some fun in the rain,
But when I got out, in both my feet, I felt a terrible pain!

My toes were clicking and snapping, my feet went round and round,
My wellie boots then twinkled, and lifted me off the ground!

Higher and higher they carried me, high up to the sky,
I didn't have time to worry because I realised I could fly!

I whooshed and swooped and twirled around
Higher and higher above the ground.

I wondered if my mum was worried about me
She probably wanted me back for tea.

I then started to fall down, lower and lower,
Gently swaying slower and slower.

Lower than the birds and lower than the trees
And then I landed slap bang on my knees.

I lifted myself up and stood on the ground
And then I heard a nice sweet sound.

'Tom, Tom, you've come back to me!
I knew you wouldn't miss your tea.

Come and sit down, take a seat
And for goodness sake have something to eat.'

That was my mum wondering where I had been,
I had the muckiest wellies she had ever seen.

She gave my boots a nice polish and put them by the door,
I'd like to go again one day but for now I'm staying on the floor!

Alina Seymore-Smith (11)
Castle Hill Middle School

Autumn Time

A utumn can be sunny
U ltimately, autumn, can be useful
T he days are getting shorter
U gly winds come to daunt us
M ums keep the garden tidy
N ights are getting much longer

T ime for a harvest festival
I am having a great time
M y conkers are powerful
E verybody loves autumn times, even me!

Chloe Tabor (10)
Castle Hill Middle School

Owl Poem

The owl flies silently by the light of the moon
It is a graceful bird of prey.
It has the softest feathers in the universe
And flies by night not day.

The owl is a very good hunter
Thanks to its 3D hearing.
So it can pinpoint the sounds from far away
And can hear what is creeping.

The owl was accused of witchcraft
And pictured with Harry Potter.
It flies with all its grace and speed
And along house roofs it does totter.

Nathanael Smalley (8)
Chilton Community Primary School

Owl Poem

Owls have very good hearing
During the day and the night,
They usually stay up when it's dark
And usually sleep in the light.

They like to eat lots of mice
And don't forget the rats,
Swooping in the sky
Not looking for tabby cats.

Joseph Wilson (8)
Chilton Community Primary School

Owl

Owls like to come out at night
But not really the light.
Owls like nice things to eat
Like rats and mice and rabbits.
When the sunshine comes out,
The owls sleep in their cosy nests being very quiet.

Grace Wharton Richardson (8)
Chilton Community Primary School

My Flight Tonight

As the sun sets I wake up ready for my flight tonight
My feathers are white as I fly silently through the black lonely night.
I see a packet of rice but I would prefer some mice.
I sit on my branch and glance at the stars as the cars drive past me.
As the sun creeps over the hills I sit in my tree and go to sleep
waiting for the next night.

Rosa Heard (8)
Chilton Community Primary School

Happiness

Happiness is bright yellow.
It tastes like juicy lemons.
Happiness is the smell of joy and laughter in a happy house
with loads of children.
It sounds really happy like everyone's laughing in a bedroom.
It feels like you're going to blow up with happiness and joy.

Rachel West (10)
College Heath Middle School

Love

Love is a deep pink like a first sunset.
It tastes like warm apple pie just cooked
And smells like a red rose just bloomed.
It looks like a rose garden in the middle of the night.
It sounds like a bird humming in the front of the window.
It feels wonderful like winning the lottery.

Hailey Cope (10)
College Heath Middle School

Excitement

Excitement is red.
It tastes like pasta and it smells lush.
Excitement looks like watching England play football and it sounds
like the national anthem.
Excitement feels like watching banger racing.

Zac Redman (11)
College Heath Middle School

Love

Love smells like a chocolate fountain all through the night
I follow the smell without making a fight.
Love smells like a sweet red rose with little drips of rain.
It tastes like a potion of love starting your body all over again.
It doesn't make you feel upset; it makes you feel happy instead.
It sounds like some water making its way down the stream
And it feels like a soft blanket of red fur.

Naomi Roberts (10)
College Heath Middle School

Love

Love is red.
Love tastes warm.
Love smells fresh and looks like the sun.
Love sounds beautiful.
Love feels like emotions throbbing through the air.

Joe Brown (10)
College Heath Middle School

Anger

Anger is red.
It tastes like a hot dog and smells like D&G men's perfume.
Anger looks like the Devil and sounds like a bomb going off.
Anger smells like a pizza, it feels like pain.

Max Hough (11)
College Heath Middle School

Excitement

Excitement is orange.
It tastes like an orange.
It smells like happiness.
It sounds like laughing.
It looks like a smile.
It feels like cats purring.

Zoe Hayward (10)
College Heath Middle School

Love

Love is deep red.
Love tastes like melted chocolate.
Love smells like sweet roses.
Love looks like red skies.
Love sounds like singing birds.
Love makes me feel happy.

Kasey Grossman (10)
College Heath Middle School

Love

Love is deep red.
Love tastes like dark chocolate.
Love smells like the air.
Love looks like boys and girls.
Love sounds like whistling birds.
Love feels like joy.

Amy Phipps (10)
College Heath Middle School

Hate

Hate is pitch-black.
Hate tastes like rotten cheese.
Hate smells like poison gas.
Hate looks like a pitch-black alleyway.
Hate sounds like charging bulls.
Hate feels like a rock falling on your head.

Robbie Gove (9)
College Heath Middle School

Anger

The colour of anger is red.
It tastes like a burnt stick.
It smells like a burning fire.
It looks like a devil.
It sounds like a crackle of fire and sticks.
It feels like burning your fingers on hot toast.

Connor Coomber (9)
College Heath Middle School

Joy

Joy is bright blue.
It tastes like fresh lavender
And smells like shiny apples.
Joy looks like a bunch of roses.
It sounds like birds tweeting and feels so, so soft.

Ben Cole (9)
College Heath Middle School

Excitement

Excitement is deep blue.
It tastes like a Whopper from Burger King.
It smells like Dominos pizza.
It looks like Old Trafford at full capacity.
It sounds like all the football fans are singing, 'Glory, glory Man United.'
It feels like you're in Heaven.

Daniel Flatt (9)
College Heath Middle School

Joy

Joy is as bright as gold and tastes like strawberry smoothies.
Joy smells like popcorn all sweet and nice
And looks like a peaceful lake all through the night.
Joy is the sound of laughter all through the day
And feels like happiness for all the people throughout the world.

Rosie Hulbert (10)
College Heath Middle School

Anger

Anger tastes like rotten tomatoes melting.
Anger is deep black.
Anger smells like horse poop.
Anger looks like the Devil's flames.
Anger sounds like someone shooting.

Joe Harrison (9)
College Heath Middle School

Anger

Anger is as red as a blazing fire.
It tastes like hot volcano sauce.
It smells like smoke.
It looks like a bomb.
It sounds like people screaming.
It feels like a bullet hitting you in the head at full speed.

Ashden Drew (9)
College Heath Middle School

Hate

Hate is grey.
Hate tastes like snot.
Hate smells like a bonfire.
Hate looks like a herd of antelope.
Hate sounds like someone crying.
Hate feels like being cut open.

Danny Gibson (9)
College Heath Middle School

Joy

Joy is dark purple.
It tastes like a banana with melted chocolate inside it.
Joy smells like nice Chinese ribs on the barbeque on a hot sunny day.
It sounds like everybody cheering in a stadium with a hint of an echo.

Nathan Almond (9)
College Heath Middle School

Loneliness

Loneliness is a sorrow grey.
It tastes like dirt being kicked at you.
It smells like the bad breath of people laughing at you.
It looks like a big black cloud over you.
It sounds like laughter.
It feels like humiliation.

James Morton (9)
College Heath Middle School

Love

Love is a pink heart beating.
Love tastes like candyfloss.
Love smells like one hundred perfumes.
Love looks like a big hug.
Love sounds like big red kisses.
Love feels like holding a big red ruby.

Danny Ryan (9)
College Heath Middle School

Anger

Anger is the colour red.
Anger tastes like rotten eggs.
Anger smells like smelly socks.
Anger looks like smoke.
Anger sounds like fire.
Anger feels like blood.

Ben Nolan (9)
College Heath Middle School

Love

Love is bright pink.
Love tastes like mint Vienetta.
Love smells like a deep red rose.
Love looks like a gold wedding ring.
Love sounds like angels singing.
Love feels like a heart pumping.

Owen Till (9)
College Heath Middle School

Freedom

Freedom is the colour of fresh green grass
And smells like fresh leaves growing on the trees.
It sounds like new baby birds tweeting.
It feels like expressing our feelings.
Freedom is the best.

Miles Stiddard (10)
College Heath Middle School

Love

Love is pink; it is the taste of sweets.
Love smells like melted chocolate and a lovely banana split.
It sounds like kissing
Love feels like having a massage.

Connor Knight (9)
College Heath Middle School

Sadness

Sadness is a deep blue sea.
It tastes like disgusting medicine
And it smells like wet rotten apples.
Sadness looks like hail, rain, storm and thunder.
It sounds like booming hurricanes.
It feels like a friend upset.

Luke Day (9)
College Heath Middle School

Love

Love is as pink as a rose.
It tastes like the sweetest sweet.
It smells like a rare flower.
Love looks like chocolate.
It sounds like angels and birds tweeting.
Love feels like a hot bath.

Harry Coldwell (9)
College Heath Middle School

Anger

Anger is deep red.
It tastes like rotten eggs.
It looks like an evil monster.
It sounds like a herd of cows.
It feels like you're being stepped on.

Ashley Pinner (9)
College Heath Middle School

Wanted: A Sharing Person

You must be . . .
As funny as a clown bashing into the wall
As loving as my mum wiping up my tears
As lively as a puppy playing with a ball
As caring as my uncle helping me face my fears
As cuddly as a teddy, furry against my face
As thoughtful as my dad helping me tie my lace.

Emma Skoulding (8)
Crowfoot Community Primary School

Wanted: A Sharing Person

You must be . . .
As caring as a loving mother
As helpful as a teacher helping me with my work
As gentle as a newborn baby
As kind as my mum helping me with my homework.

Michael Clarke (8)
Crowfoot Community Primary School

Sharing

In my family we like to share,
Funny songs, smart ideas, happy days
And a cake as big as the world!

With my friends I like to play,
Clever cartwheels, Nintendo DS, great sleepovers
And a chocolate as big as a house!

Vanna Dodd (9)
Crowfoot Community Primary School

Sharing

In my family we like to share,
Playing like pirates digging up gold.
In the summer it's really hot,
In the winter we share because it's cold.

When we're at home we bake some cakes
Sharing together makes it quick.
Robert is funny, he makes Mum cross
Like a clown juggling with sticks.

Laura Holmes (7)
Crowfoot Community Primary School

Sharing

With my friends I like to play
Cool skipping, funny songs, Mr Wolf
And shopping in town.

Lauren King (8)
Crowfoot Community Primary School

Chocolate

Milk chocolate is so delicious to eat
Every day, why not have a treat!
Dark and white chocolate too,
Some with nuts just for you.
Large bars, small bars, sweets in jar,
Crunchies, Twix, Ripples and Mars.
Chocolate to eat,
Chocolate to drink,
Chocolate to make your dreams.

Rachael McMaster (10)
Elm Tree Middle School

Fireworks

Here I am at the show
Where the fireworks boom, crackle and glow.
As high as the glittery stars they will fly
Up, up away into the dark night sky.
As hot as the sun they will burn
They do different moves like pops, twists and turn.
But most of all I love the Catherine wheel
Which really gives me that Guy Fawkes feel.

Kirsty Clarke (10)
Elm Tree Middle School

Fear

Fear is like the black sky at midnight.
It reminds me of the worst nightmare I have ever had.
It smells like rats lying dead on the floor.
It looks like a giant monster coming towards your house.
It sounds like big footsteps stepping on the floor.
It tastes like eating chocolate in bed alone.
It feels like being trapped in a dungeon forever long.

Rory Grant (9)
Elm Tree Middle School

Anger

Anger is red like a red car.
Anger smells like steamy smoke.
Anger reminds me of murder.
Anger looks like you're going to burst.
Anger feels like you're hard and bumpy.
Anger tastes like very hot chillies.
Anger sounds like a foghorn.

Daniel Minshaw (9)
Elm Tree Middle School

Love

Love is pink like the sunset by the beach.
Love looks like happiness.
Love feels like a gentle kiss and makes you feel young.
Love tastes like smooth light chocolate.
Love sounds like a quiet harp.
Love smells like a warm hot chocolate.
Love reminds me of the summer.

Maisie Wright (9)
Elm Tree Middle School

Hate

Hate is grey like the greyest sky.
It smells like fire.
It sounds like horror.
It feels like my worst enemy standing in front of me.
It tastes like something has gone wrong.
It reminds me of anger.
It looks like the world has shrunk.

Hollie Marjoram (9)
Elm Tree Middle School

Happiness

Happiness is yellow like the big bright sun.
It feels light and soft like a newborn kitten.
Happiness sounds sweet as music.
It smells like cupcakes out of the oven.
Happiness tastes sweet with a touch of Heaven.
It reminds me of home.

Toni-Ann Field (9)
Elm Tree Middle School

Love

Love is red like a heart beating.
It feels like romance.
It reminds me of strawberries.
It tastes like jam.
It looks like a playground.
It sounds like soft music.
It smells like a juicy kiwi fruit.

PaulJørgen Jackson (9)
Elm Tree Middle School

My Poem For Anger

Anger is dark red like when you're angry.
It feels like your head is going to explode.
It tastes like sick.
It smells like fire.
It looks like a volcano erupting.
It sounds like thunder and lightning.
It reminds me of my sister punching me.

Thomas Godfrey-Collins (10)
Elm Tree Middle School

Fear

Fear is black like the darkest sky.
It feels like someone is watching you.
It sounds like a heart beating.
It tastes like poisoned water.
It smells like rotten mould.
It reminds me of a serial killer.
It looks like death.

Kristian Zajdek Haverson (9)
Elm Tree Middle School

Anger

Anger is black like a storm crashing together.
It sounds like lightning striking.
It smells like burning lightning.
It looks like black explosions.
It reminds me of volcanoes.
It tastes like hot air.
It feels like I'm trapped in a room and I will never get out.

Katey Oven (9)
Elm Tree Middle School

Love

Love is like a red rose.
It looks like a red crystal beaming.
It smells like a world of butterflies and flowers.
It reminds me of a wedding.
It feels like people having a lovely time.
It tastes like lovely oozing melted chocolate.
It sounds like a violin playing joyful music.

Catherine Baldwin (9)
Elm Tree Middle School

Hate

Hate is red like a heart broken.
It tastes like black blood dripping swiftly from the zombie leg.
It looks like a bully beating up a boy and snapping his wrist.
It smells like dead people in a coffin.
It reminds me of my brother being disgusting at the table.
It feels like a ghost, at night, wants to kill me.
It sounds like a wolf outside my bedroom window howling.

Lawson Altham (9)
Elm Tree Middle School

Fear

Fear is yellow like a banana.
It feels like snowy cold wind.
It looks like cold frost on the end of my nose.
It reminds me of the time I was left alone.
It tastes like yellow snow.
It sounds like someone crying.
It smells like the dirty mud on the bottom of my shoe.

Emily-Rose Powell (9)
Elm Tree Middle School

Love

Love is red like a pretty flower.
It looks like a red rose.
It reminds me of a holiday.
It tastes like chocolate.
It sounds like someone getting married.
It feels like a relaxing soft pillow.
It smells like a box of chocolate.

Katie Williams (9)
Elm Tree Middle School

Happiness

Happiness is pink like skin
It feels like a calm sea.
It tastes like sweets.
It looks like people playing with each other.
It smells like soap.
It reminds me of my brother playing with me.
It sounds like laughter.

Sophie Blaza (9)
Elm Tree Middle School

Fear

Fear is orange like a scared lonely cat.
It smells like people who are scared and cold.
It reminds me of bad memories.
It tastes like when I'm sick.
It looks like a colossal cloud.
It sounds like someone screaming out for help.
It feels like a cold, hard wall.

Tiffany Griffiths (9)
Elm Tree Middle School

Love

Love is red like a rose.
It reminds me of romance.
It tastes like sugar roses.
It looks like the most wonderful things.
It smells like rose perfume.
It sounds like a water fountain.
It feels like an angel touching you.

Emily Reeve (9)
Elm Tree Middle School

Fear

Fear is like an ice cube.
It tastes like sweat each day.
It looks like scary faces.
It reminds me of that day.
It smells like sweat and vinegar.
It sounds like children's screams.
It feels like people playing on other children's games.

Emma-Constance Tanoe
Elm Tree Middle School

Fear

Fear is white like a ghost.
It tastes like something dry and salty.
It looks like crisp white hair.
It feels like a nasty pain in your stomach.
It reminds me of a horrid nightmare you just want to wake up from.
It sounds like someone screaming.
It smells like rotten eggs.

Olivia Thomson (10)
Elm Tree Middle School

Anger

Anger is red like lava and magma.
Anger sounds like an elephant rampaging through a busy street.
Anger feels like nails stuck in your ears.
Anger tastes like lukewarm Coke.
Anger smells like hair alight.
Anger reminds me of my annoying brother.
Anger looks like the Devil's face.

Connor Calver (10)
Elm Tree Middle School

Fun

Fun is like climbing trees.
It looks like boys playing football.
It reminds me of trampolines.
It smells like cheese.
It sounds like Mega Munchers.
It tastes like sausages.

Charlie Harrison-Reeve (10)
Elm Tree Middle School

Golf Balls, Golf Balls

We're small, we're round
You hit us off the ground.
Golf balls, golf balls
No one can see how far we go.
Golf balls, golf balls, we hit the hole,
We sometimes hit a mole!
Golf balls, golf balls
The mole, the mole,
Stops us getting a goal!
Golf balls, golf balls.

Kale Brown (9)
Elm Tree Middle School

Anger

Anger is red like a fiery god.
It smells like sweat.
It looks like ash.
It tastes like very spicy chilli.
It feels like heat.
It reminds me of Hell.
It sounds like crackling and growling.

Scott Barwood (10)
Elm Tree Middle School

Sadness

Sadness is brown or black like dancing night.
It reminds me of crying.
It sounds like shouting.
It looks like you're falling out.
It feels like cold.
It tastes like vinegar.
It smells like chopped onions.

Deanna Fox (10)
Elm Tree Middle School

Sadness

Sadness is a pool of tears
Forming a puddle at my feet.
It is losing a family member
Or a special pet.
It feels like a dark cloud is hanging over my head
Sticking to me like glue.
It is a sad story
Everyone throws in the bin.
A rotten cabbage
Making the air stink.
Sadness is a snail
Feeling very sluggish.
It is a mosquito bite
Stinging me like mad.
It is a child
Feeling very upset.
It feels like a little wet river
Trickling down my face.
Sadness is the last chocolate from the selection pack.

Lily Alger (10)
Elm Tree Middle School

Sadness

Sadness is a bitter lemon
All dull with misery.
Sadness is a lonely day
With depression and never happy.
Tears make a pool of water
That will never dry up and go away.
Cry, cry, it will never help
The drops run down your cheek
You alone, locked up and the key thrown away.

Brodie Lock (11)
Elm Tree Middle School

If The World Was Crazy

If the world was crazy, you know what I'd eat?
A trifle tart with some smelly feet and some chocolate meat,
Some roasted pies and some jam eyes,
A nice thick coat with a goat,
An orange coat with a boat,
A paper boat with a jam tart coat,
Some smelly shoes and some great news,
That's what I'd eat if the world was crazy.

If the world was crazy, you know what I'd wear?
I'd wear a chocolate éclair,
Some marshmallow shoes and the news
And I'd read a book full of shoes.
I'd call the boys Suzy and I'd call the girls Harry,
I'd talk through my ears and would always carry a bag full of jam.

If the world was crazy, you know what I'd do?
I'd swim in the ocean and drink a potion,
I'd fly through the air and have a pear,
I'd eat the pear and go to the fair
When I met somebody I'd say, 'Could you do my hair?'
And when they went I'd say, 'Give me a pear!'
So then I'd be crazy queen if the world was crazy

Rebecca Baldwin (9)
Elm Tree Middle School

Anger

Anger is black like a bull.
It looks like death.
It sounds like you are going down.
It smells like rotten eggs.
It feels like a fiery hole.
It reminds me of my mum pointing her finger at me.
It tastes like chilli peppers.

Jack Capps-Jenner (10)
Elm Tree Middle School

The Kangaroo And The Emu

(Based on 'The Owl and the Pussy Cat' by Edward Lear)

The kangaroo and the emu went to space
In a wonderful big red rocket,
They took some cheese and lots of peas
All in the kangaroo's pocket.
The kangaroo sat on his shoe
And sang to the small emu.
'Oh fluffy emu, oh fluffy emu,
How wonderfully fluffy you are,
You are,
You are
How wonderfully fluffy you are.'
'Kangaroo,' said the emu
'You make my heart bounce
Oh let us be wed, in my garden shed.'
And off they went with a spring and a pounce
They walked up the path with a giggle and a laugh
To the shed with the big pink door,
Pink door,
Pink door
The shed with the big pink door.
After the do, they went to the zoo and danced in the monkey's cage
They ate some cake, on a silver plate by the edge of a moonlit pond.
A year passed and then at last, a baby eroo was born,
Was born,
Was born,
A baby eroo was born.

Lydia Chilvers (9)
Elm Tree Middle School

The Beach And The Sea

The beach is an open space with giant crabs
And whistling singers singing in the grass.
The sea carries death in the giant boats sunk for life.
The sea twists in the mist; it's a snake on the sand.
The sand is a mountain range of many dunes.
The waves are springs bouncing onto the sand
Making foam froth along the shore
Enjoy the icy delight from the ice cream van, a cooling balm on a hot day.

Joshua Ward (10)
Elm Tree Middle School

Sadness

A tear is a river dripping down your cheek
You're alone with no one with you.
It overwhelms you like a dark cloud.
It tastes like a bitter lemon.
Feelings of emotions running high,
Your stomach hurts like there is no tomorrow.
Head's pounding, like a herd of elephants
Depression's clinging to you.

Laura Hadingham (10)
Elm Tree Middle School

The Beach

The beach is a lion hunting for its prey.
He roars at the children while tearing the fish with his dreaded jaws.
A giant stripped as the waves come and go.
In the winter the beach is a gritty ice cream that nobody can eat.
The pebbles are marbles than nobody can roll.
The beach is a sleeping giant waiting for the sunlight.

Elenna Smither (10)
Elm Tree Middle School

Sadness

A tiny river dripping down your cheek
Your eyes swell up with them.
It is like a big black cloud floating above you,
Sadness makes you feel trapped
Lost, in a lonely room
With a million bolts on the doors.
Sadness lurks around the world
Wanting to lash out at you at any time.
It makes itself at home inside your body
It will drag you to Hell,
Lead you to it and *boom!*
You will never open your eyes with the slightest piece of happiness or
the slightest smile,
Say goodbye to it all.

Danielle Thomson (10)
Elm Tree Middle School

The Sea Is . . .

Calm and relaxing and is never hungry,
mad and crazy and always hungry,
ill and weak and never eaten anything,
a wild spitting camel,
a giant coming from the top
he roars at the children on the beach.
Stripped as the sand bank comes and goes,
a mad snake twisting and curling around,
twisting in the ugly mists with its snake-like body,
a huge monster,
a giant killing everyone,
the beast of the beach.

Abigail Cowley (10)
Elm Tree Middle School

The Great Footy Match

The score was nil-nil
Who would score the winning goal?
The ball was running across that pitch
The goal was standing still.
The ball happily walked into the goal.
The scoreboard excitedly changed to one-nil.
The goal jumped up frantically in excitement
All the football boots sprinted round the pitch desperately.
The football hopped across the pitch.
A football boot got it started running down the wing and put a cross in
Smash! One-one!
The scoreboard frantically changed and the whistle blew itself
Final score, one-one.

Jack Ellwood (10)
Elm Tree Middle School

Sadness

Sadness is a sour lemon.
Sadness is a pool of tears.
Sadness is the last leaf falling.
Sadness is a wilting flower.
Sadness is a broken friendship.
Sadness is a stack of homework.

Micah Trevor-Massey (10)
Elm Tree Middle School

Love

Love is red like two people going out.
Love smells like rose flowers.
Love feels like two people together forever.
Love tastes like eating chocolate.
Love reminds me of your boyfriend taking you out for tea.

Charmaine Burrows (11)
Elm Tree Middle School

Fireworks

It came to one beautiful night
Where the sky lit up with a crackle and a fight
The fireworks were coming, coming soon tonight.
Whoosh! Bang! There goes another,
Crack! Pop! One scared my brother.
They flew through the sky with anger and rage
They were fighting and battling for the old human face.
'The sky is mine,' the firework roared
The ground is mine, the sparkler thought.
Now that night has ended for good
The fireworks are gone and I say they should
But soon they'll be coming, coming again
With anger and rage so I'm going in my den.

Toinen Phillips (11)
Elm Tree Middle School

The Wind Turbine

An eagle in the sky watching you
Flapping its wings madly
Drumming them against the clouds
As it sweeps through the air
Looking over you, staring you right in the eyes
But still drumming its wings against the clouds
Still sweeping through the sky.

Polly Draper (10)
Elm Tree Middle School

The Sea

He roars at children playing on the beach, munching on their buckets
Once he left a toy on the beach, next day it was gone.
He spits on rocks, destroys small stones.
One day a year, in the summer, he is friendly and brings all fish for human eyes to see.

Chantelle Cunningham (10)
Elm Tree Middle School

Fountains

Mountain-high squirts from a spitting camel
Laughing hyenas running through getting wet, having fun
Unexpected squirts
Near the beach
Plenty of ice cream
Zoo of people
Laid back lions
Is it now?
Is it late?
Will they squirt up when I am through
Lightning cheetahs springing through
Rapid racers running round
Never-ending
Run, run, run
Wet, wet, wet,
Quick, quick, quick!

Olivia Peat (11)
Elm Tree Middle School

A Starry Night

The owls were hooting
I didn't know what I was doing
The wolves howled,
The cat scowled,
The sun was down
I had a frown
Late down town
There was no sound
The bats were dancing, how very odd!
I feel like eating a piece of cod.
The fireflies were out today
Now I think I have to say
The stars were twinkling above my head
I think it's time to go to bed.

Natasha Chan (11)
Elm Tree Middle School

Soldiers

One sunny morning
Soldiers were planning
To blow up the forest
With tanks and guns.

A massive explosion
Two million lights
Bears growling
Fires as hot as a trillion suns.

Now most of the creatures
In the forest
Were burned to a frizzle
But some escaped.

Foxes and mice
Rabbits and moles
Because they all went
Underground where
It's as cold as a freezer.

Wesley Cane (10)
Elm Tree Middle School

The Butter Butterfly

The butterfly was yellow and small
Her wings fluttering everywhere.
But to my surprise she was tall;
She landed safely on the ground
And gave me a little grin.
I felt happier and happier every time
She flew up on my chin.
Looking up at me singing a song
She fell asleep all night long.
High, high up in the sky
But now I say, 'Goodbye my little butterfly.'

Emma Spore (10)
Elm Tree Middle School

I Will Put In The Box

(Based on 'Magic Box' by Kit Wright)

I will put in my box . . .
A fox's tail, red and furry,
Some googly eyes that are scary,
A pig's tail long and curly,
A monkey's nose, big and hairy.

I will put in my box . . .
Lots of sweets that are yummy,
A kiss at bedtime from my mummy,
Man Utd football team as they are great,
My friend Aaran as he's my best mate.

I will put in my box . . .
All my thoughts that I treasure,
Playing football, that's a pleasure,
Singing songs in the shower,
My car 'cause it's got power.

Cameron Polley (9)
Elm Tree Middle School

FC

Green and scaly, a dragon's back
Tall white mouths open wide
Saviours destroy the dragon's back
With their sharp blades
An eyeball flies high in the sky
And is kicked in the dragon's ear
Visitors come and watch the dragon's death
Noise, noise, noise and cheers, cheers, cheers
Are coming from the sideline.

Aidan O'Brien (10)
Elm Tree Middle School

My Haunted Room

The bed stood as still as a lamp post,
The curtains danced in the light of the moon.
The light dazzled and shone into my room
Waking me up and giving me a fright.

The window laughed and sang a song,
The fire smiled and sang along.
The photos jumped up and down
In my haunted room.

The throw rug cried out for his mum
The drawers chewed some sticky gum
The wardrobe hopped around the place
In my haunted room

And now I go to sleep at last
For all is done and all is past.
My haunted room has gone to rest
Which I think is for the best.

Maria Read (10)
Elm Tree Middle School

The Christmas Cat

The cat was decorating her Christmas tree
She stopped and thought, *what's for tea?*
I will have tuna and milk,
Then possibly lie on my blanket made of silk.
While eating her tuna she got out her tuba
And played the samba.

She then lay on her silk blanket
And heard her neighbour and thought, *what a racket!*
The next day the sky was grey, but she said, 'Hey, it's Christmas Day
But too bad it's a rainy day.'

Alice Edwards (10)
Elm Tree Middle School

Fireworks

A rocket is fat and big as an elephant
Glitter is shiny as a display
The kaboom is like a bomb going off
They are fast fireworks
A firework goes *bang!*
Fireworks are pretty colours in the sky
Flames are like fire
Fireworks go flash so brightly
The fireworks crackle when they are lit
Loads of flashing
Loads of lights going on
Some fireworks are silent
Fireworks, crackling noises
Some fireworks are pink, purple and all different colours and sizes
Some fireworks go *whoosh* to fly.

Alysha Holmes-Thrower (10)
Elm Tree Middle School

The Weekly Bone

Once there was a little dog
A nose as soft as silk,
He had a bone for every week
And loved to drink his milk.
He had lots of friends with lots of bones
They hid them under sticks and stone.
Then one day the neighbour said,
'Do you want to play?'
'I'd surely love to,' said the dog
'But it's not that kind of day.
'That's OK,' said the neighbour
'I'll just go and play with the other neighbours
Then he'll take me to the park
Then I will continue to bark.'

Millie Dilworth (10)
Elm Tree Middle School

The Guinea Pig

The guinea pig looked at me
She was waiting for her yummy tea.
She waved and clapped
Stood straight and flapped
And then she ran away
To go off and play.

The guinea pig came running back
But she wasn't alone; she had a friend with her.
It was another guinea pig
They started to dance
And I started to glance,
Then they both said bye
But I wonder why?
Why did they have to go,
Oh well, it was a good show.

Darcy Grimmer (10)
Elm Tree Middle School

The Evil Fish

A fish was looking at me
In an extraordinary way
'Hello Sir' I think he was trying to say.
Him and I were looking at the clock
Tick-tock, tick-tock
OK, I have no time to waste
Just to see how he tastes
I tried and I tried and tried
For me it did not work
For he looking at me in a smirk
Really, I tried and I tried and I tried.

Ben King (10)
Elm Tree Middle School

The Weather Poem

Rain is wet
Sun is hot
Lightning is frightening
But snow is not.

Clouds can bring rain,
Clouds can bring snow,
Clouds can move very fast
When a strong wind does blow.

Kyle Rushmere (10)
Elm Tree Middle School

Sweets In A Jar

Sweets are delicious to eat
So colourful and bright
Lighter and lighter
The more times you eat
Smells nice
Tastes nice
Looks nice
They are big, fat and juicy.

Rebecca Clements (10)
Elm Tree Middle School

The Weather Is Like Me

The sun is as bright as my smile.
The snow is as white as my teeth.
The thunder is as loud as my shouting.
The wind is as strong as me whistling.
I am as cold as a box of ice cubes.
The rain is as wet as the tears from my eyes.

Daniel Clarke (10)
Elm Tree Middle School

World War II

I'm in a bomb shelter hiding
From the bombs outside,
A bomb comes down right above me.
I go outside to try and spot some Germans
I see one, I move closer . . .
The blood on the grass looks like poppies.
I shoot him, he survives.
So I turn around and it's the end for me.

Joe Andrews (10)
Elm Tree Middle School

Trees

Sun shines and the trees stand still
Come autumn time, her leaves will spill
The trees now waving side to side
No leaves at all, nowhere to hide.
Spring again, another year
The tree's alive, new leaves appear
The tree's still smiling, she's full of glee
Now shady places for you and me.

Sophie Newson (10)
Elm Tree Middle School

Firework

Fireworks, fireworks, I just love fireworks
They are colourful and loud just like me
Fireworks, fireworks, they make loud bangs
And for food we eat toffee apples
Toffee apples, toffee apples
I love eating toffee apples, they are the best.

Harry McNicholas (10)
Elm Tree Middle School

The Sun

It is like a dragon burning fire
When it gets dark it flies away
Like a crystal ball in the sky
A ball of fire that burns your eyes.

Warm and sticky all day long
Like a ball of lava in the sky
Extremely warm on a cold day

When we wake up in the morning
In the sticky afternoon

Some people say it is like a firework
Exploding in the sky
Like a never-ending light bulb

Far away in the galaxy
With all of the other planets
Floating behind the clouds.

Weston Taylor (9)
Laureate CP School

The Sun

The sun is like a wild ball in the solar system shining and sparkling
in space.

It's the biggest planet in the dark sky.
It feels like a scorching oven, it has flames everywhere
So if you touch it you will have a red hand.
You see the sun in daytime and at noon so you only see it sometimes.
People say it's a sphere of flames; it's a ball of fire.
It's in space and the solar system.

Jake Paterson (8)
Laureate CP School

The Sun

A shining crystal ball in the crystal-blue sky
An orange in the deep blue sky
A football being kicked into the sea-like sky.

It feels warm and cosy
Hot against the skin
A ring of fire

We see it in the warm times
Even in the summer
Also at hot times

People say that it has a burning temperature
Lines around its circle
It lowers when the sky is black

Millions of miles away from the ground
Burning behind the clouds
Peeping through quietly.

Ryan Tanner (8)
Laureate CP School

The Sun

A ball on fire like a face in the sky.
Warming my cold skin, fire burning back, it makes the future feel warm.
In the burning desert in summertime in Africa.
Sometimes very hot, it makes you sweat wen it's burning in the sky
sparkling in the sky.
Behind the clouds, up in the sky floating and shining.

Daniel Woelfl (8)
Laureate CP School

The Sun

A huge, golden bowling bowl,
Turning to make sparkles
To light the whole planet.

A match that tans my cold skin,
As I take my jumper off
Boiling and scorching me.

On holiday near the equator
Or peeping through your curtains
To keep you warm.

A mighty, shiny plate
That turns in the cloudy sky
To cook the planets.

It takes months
To get to the hottest place in the universe.

Lily Greenwood (9)
Laureate CP School

The Sun

It's like fireworks bursting in the sky.
It looks like a burning ring of fire and lava exploding.
It feels like it's burning skin, melting it.
It's warming my skin.
We see the sun on very hot days in really hot deserts.
People say that it looks like a crystal ball.
It is a big ball of gas; it is in dark space floating everywhere,
It's up in the big blue sky.

Shaun Keeley (8)
Laureate CP School

Untitled

It's like a dragon breathing fire in the sky.
When it gets dark it flies away in the night sky.
It's a golden ball on fire that hangs in the sky.
It's also a gorgeous juicy orange burning.
It feels like a bonfire in the sky coming closer and closer.
It also feels like an oven burning, like a light bulb burning your hands,
We see it when it's hot and sweaty on boiling hot afternoons.
People say it's a big smiling face burning in the sky.
It's the face of fire.
It's millions of school buses stacked up.
It's millions of miles away.

Simone Warren (8)
Laureate CP School

The Sun

The sun is like a crystal ball in the blue sky making the earth hot,
warming my blood.
It feels like fire burning my skin making me sweat.
I see it on a lovely sunny day peeping through my curtains.
People say it's a living creature, a fire-breathing dragon.
It is burning up the atmosphere, floating behind white fluffy clouds.

Thomas Spinks (8)
Laureate CP School

Heart

I am locked away silently
I am broken and lost in a world of sadness
Till I meet the one that longs to be with me.
I will start to beat my same old tune.
I need to find the one; I am bored of waiting now
So I have stopped beating, now he has gone.

Robert Johnson & Guy Barraclough (10)
Mellis CE (VC) Primary School

Who Am I?

I can fly high in the sky
I can watch people going to work
I'm sometimes pretty
I have a repeated pattern on my wings
People see me as I fly
I come in different colours like red, yellow, blue, green
I have seen the world many times
I have changed from a caterpillar to this animal
I have nice friends from the world
I am a butterfly.

Sophie Cooper (10)
Mellis CE (VC) Primary School

The Life Bringer

I light up the Earth with my spectacular shine
I take over the world using that glow of mine.
Children play when I am around
Adults smile when they see my glow in the morning.
The wonderful world would not exist if I wasn't around.
I am the most important thing on Earth, I am Sun.

Emily Bix (10)
Mellis CE (VC) Primary School

The Shiver Bringer!

I fall from above mysteriously
I miss the Earth, it's a warm place
Until I settle once again
I return every year
I turn the Earth into a soft silky carpet under your feet.
I am Snow!

Georgia Pearson (10)
Mellis CE (VC) Primary School

The Secret Keeper

I am kept in a dark musty room,
I am opened rarely,
Only my owner knows my code
Inside me there are precious things.
Neither fire nor water may ever hurt me.
I have skin of steel.
I am more complicated than anything electronic.
I have a key, the best in history,
I am a safe.

Jack Walton (10)
Mellis CE (VC) Primary School

The Rich Time Capsule

I remember being put away
I live in the ground longing for a better purpose.
I am afraid of not seeing light ever again.
I can live for centuries.
I hope that one day I will be opened
I am a treasure chest.

Liam Fairweather (10)
Mellis CE (VC) Primary School

Stars

I glimmer in the sky.
I glide in the sky.
I am a thing that lights the sky.
I have met other stars.
I remember the world when it began.

Jake Moon (10)
Mellis CE (VC) Primary School

Tree

I feel the wind
I touch the sky
I clasp the solid earth
I give shade to all around me
My fingers are open to birds
I am covered with the colour green
I am small in spring
I am thriving in summer
I am dripping in autumn
I am dark in winter
I am Tree.

Francesca Daw (10)
Mellis CE (VC) Primary School

A Sunflower

The sunflower is bright like the sun
Its stem is a tall tree
The petals are pretty like a butterfly
The white roots are a plain wire
The stem is strong like a rock
The head is a black tile
The wiggly roots are like worms
The sunflower is a beautiful picture.

Laguna Allum (9)
Mellis CE (VC) Primary School

Untitled

I live in a ring next to sapphire and ruby.
I see her fingers stretched out in front of me.
I have been worn hundreds of times,
I am a diamond.

Hannah Gudde (10)
Mellis CE (VC) Primary School

Haunted House

A haunted house is a walking nightmare.
It is a dark hole.
It sounds like a werewolf howling.
It is a homeless house.
A haunted house makes me shiver like a tree in the breeze.
My legs wobble like jelly.
My heart beats fast as a train.
My teeth rattle like chains.
My body is as light as a balloon.
Boo! The ghost haunting the house is me!

Tristyn Tunmer (9)
Mellis CE (VC) Primary School

Ring Of Guilt

Guilt is grey like a raincloud following you.
It sounds like a balloon popping in your head.
It tastes like a poison that continues in your mouth.
It smells like a chocolate that is impossible to reach.
It feels like a ring of darkness getting bigger in your stomach.
It reminds me of ice slowly creeping up on you.

Luke Barraclough (8)
Mellis CE (VC) Primary School

A Lamb

It is as a cloud
The fluffy lamb is a bouncing trampoline
It is as soft as a stuffed dog
The tiny lamb is running about in the field
It is as tiny as a toy cat
The cute ball of fluff is jumping on her mum.

Stephen Wicks (9)
Mellis CE (VC) Primary School

Ballet Dancer

She is a cloud in the sky
She is rain falling
She is thunder creaking
She is wind floating
She is a tree swaying in the wind
She is a wave moving
She is a sun sinking and ballet dancer is a sparkle in a star.

Mollie Drummond (10)
Mellis CE (VC) Primary School

Darkness

Darkness is the colour of black tarmac.
It sounds like a werewolf howling.
It tastes like rotten eggs.
It smells like a dustbin lorry.
It looks like your worst nightmare.
It feels like you're without a shadow
And it reminds me of the day I lost my pet.

Elsa Thurlow (9)
Mellis CE (VC) Primary School

Darkness

It reminds me of a pitch-black graveyard
It sounds like a werewolf howling.
It tastes of fear.
It looks like a pathway to nightmares.
It feels like pain.
Its colour is inky and it smells of fire.

Matthew Justice (8)
Mellis CE (VC) Primary School

Trawler

My home is the sea
I taste the salt
I smell the fish
I see the frightful waves
I wish for a good catch
I have engines the size of doors
A captain as good as no other
My nets are pulled up and I head home.

James Lazar (10)
Mellis CE (VC) Primary School

Shoes

I wish to be worn and used
But I don't want to be broken.
I like to look around the world
I've paced it many times.
I learn and see a new thing every day.
Every step means a new thing to me.
I have my own house when I'm alone
But I'm never alone, I have my twin.

Ben Roberts (10)
Mellis CE (VC) Primary School

Clouds

I am soft like a pillow on a bed
I am soaring high in the sky above the world
I watch the people moving from place to place
I wander around and stare at you
I love to watch the morning sun
I remember the waving sea
I travel the world.

Caitlin Davy (10)
Mellis CE (VC) Primary School

Olympics

Take an Olympic winner
Blend in a race
Sprinkle in a winning ceremony
And take a picture of their face
Put it in a newspaper
And sell it to the buyers
Make the winner a golden medal
And put it round their neck
Add in a laurel wreath
And place it on their head
Play their national anthem
And let the crowd applaud
There you have it
It's all done
You have a winner
And have had fun!

Mollie Robertson-Allerton (9)
Mellis CE (VC) Primary School

It's A Doggie Dog World

Bone chewer
Food eater
Kennel lover
Dozy sleeper
Treat feaster
Teddy hurter
Tail chaser
Noisy barker
Bad pooer
Bath splasher.

Robbie Scoggins (10)
Mellis CE (VC) Primary School

Motorbike

Brain squisher
Speed breaker
Road killer
Wind smasher
Motor steamer
Crash maker
Fuse batter
Seat comforter
Gear changer
Wheel hogger
Light gulper
Engine sneaker
Petrol eater
Smoke smeller.

Harrison Perry (8)
Mellis CE (VC) Primary School

Polar Bear

Fish catcher
Fluffy creature
Big killer
Seal snatcher
Warm cuddler
Heavy swimmer
Family carer
Ice scrambler
Meat eater
Cuddly lover
Teeth biter
Fish is dead.

Ella Ling (9)
Mellis CE (VC) Primary School

A Graveyard

A graveyard is a skeleton's dream.
It's a monster's wonder.
It's like a dead man's nightmare.
It's a lady's hell.
It's Big Foot's heaven.
It's like a dark hole.
It's a ghost's rose.
It's like a dying lily.
It's a caveman's starlight.
It's a cat's moonlight.
A graveyard is a spooky place
Beware the gravestones, they are in your face.
It's a ghostly fight, never go to a graveyard;
You will be gone forever and never return.

Abby Martin (9)
Mellis CE (VC) Primary School

School

It's a walking nightmare
It's no walk in the park
It's a devil's lair
It's a torture for me
It's a body without a heart
It's a clock without hands
It's a fish without a tank
It's a flattened fly
It's a board without a pen
It's a newspaper without news
It's a spider without legs
School is an endless nightmare.

Nathan Banks (9)
Mellis CE (VC) Primary School

Family

Kind lover
Heart breaker
Oven baker
Food maker
Homework helper
Money saver
Bedroom tidier
Lunchbox packer.

Rosie Bix (8)
Mellis CE (VC) Primary School

Dog

Bad pooper
Mad fighter
Cat chaser
Sneaky eater
Sniffy shouter
Bum sniffer
Sloppy licker
Deep sleeper.

Ben Shepherd (9)
Mellis CE (VC) Primary School

Schools

Teachers keep you up all day long
Doing work, not doing plays
They say to you, *no, no, no, no*
Start again it's spelt this way.

Anouk Rowlandson (9)
Mellis CE (VC) Primary School

My Dogs

At 39 Castle Street there are three dogs like angry dragons,
Maurice the Minotaur with his mighty roar
Keegan the crackpot with his horn-like call
Brady the brave, when he opens his mouth it strikes
like a thousand sewers.

Keegan is a velvet curtain
Maurice's coat is as tangled as a spider's web
Brady's coat is a stick of liquorice
What a strange bunch of dogs.

Alan Everett (9)
Mellis CE (VC) Primary School

Darkness

It looks like a dead rat.
It sounds like a wolf howling in the night.
It tastes like mouldy bread.
It smells like out of date milk.
It looks like something we have never seen.
It feels like something hairy.
It reminds me of emptiness.

Reece Lanchester (9)
Mellis CE (VC) Primary School

Love

The colour is red like roses.
It sounds like God talking to me from Heaven.
It tastes like melting chocolate in my mouth.
It smells like strawberries.
It looks like my family.
It feels like a hug from my family for the first time.
It reminds me of my friends.

Abby Dent (9)
Mellis CE (VC) Primary School

Jack Bowman, My Best Friend

First mix friendliness with being cool
Then ice with footballs and football shirts,
Next heat for twenty minutes.
For this step you can use hairspray
But it's a better taste if you use hair gel.
Sprinkle whichever you use on top of Jack,
Add one litre of jokes.
Wait ten minutes for it to rise
Then boil with kindness.
Finish off with a funny laugh
And there's your Jack Bowman, my best friend.

Aaron Fulcher (10)
Mellis CE (VC) Primary School

A Love Poem

Love is like a rainbow
Love sounds like a bird tweeting at dawn
Love tastes like a chocolate melting in your mouth
Love smells like a big rose
Love looks like a waterfall trickling down
Love feels like silk on your fingers
Love reminds me of a heart glistening red
This is the poem of love.

Daniel Brooks (9)
Mellis CE (VC) Primary School

My Mummy

My mummy is so yummy, I love my mummy.
Her skin is like a shiny apple
Her smile is like a bright ruby gemstone
Her hair is as soft as a flowing breeze
Her eyes are like sapphires sparkling like stars in the night.

Jack Turner (8)
Mellis CE (VC) Primary School

A Desert Is . . .

A desert is an unforgiving land
Where people cannot be found.
It's like a sandy trap
Where you'll find your heart will pound.

A desert is a sea of sand
Where golden pyramids stand.
It's heartless and brainless but still vicious
Where nobody will give you a hand.

A desert is a lifeless corpse
Where plants crave for water
And animals fight for life.
Travellers beware or your life may be shorter.

Emily Friar (10)
Mellis CE (VC) Primary School

Spooky Home

It's an overgrown home
It's a rotten bone
It's a stinky stench
It's a dusty bench
It's a creep for crawlies
It's a spider in the hallways
It's a big web
It's a tiny head
It's a normal bed
It's a garden shed.

Guy Campbell (9)
Mellis CE (VC) Primary School

Springtime

Spring is birds reciting poetry
While they sit in the golden oak tree.
It is a choir singing
While sitting on a bed of roses.

Spring is hugs and kisses
In a warm cosy room
It is children playing
In a park full of friendship.

Spring is an air freshener
Being sprayed in your bathroom.
It is a strawberry pavlova
Being eaten at a tea party.

Spring is people
Licking their ice creams.
It is a tune being sung in the wind.
Spring means everything!

Katherine Greenwell (10)
St Louis Catholic Middle School, Bury St Edmunds

A Football Is . . .

A football is . . .
A chequered flag scrunched up to be played with,
A ying-yang being bounced around,
A mini world waiting to be found,
A newspaper being thrown by the wind,
A polar bear curiously walking into pitch-black,
A penguin being chucked into a white net,
A zebra dizzily spinning around and around,
A football is a black and white ball.

Niall Redmond (10)
St Louis Catholic Middle School, Bury St Edmunds

Sometimes Beauty Doesn't Last Forever

She is gentle and generous,
She is cosy and warm,
She glistens like ice in the sunlight.
Snow is like a silk white blanket floating across the misty skies
And landing on the ground creating another blanket of clear
white crystal.

Snow brings joy and happiness,
Snow brings fun and games.
Snow is like sugar-coated icing on top of a cake
Her crisp coating of cream covers every window frame
From the High Street to the village store,
From the church steeple to everyone's door.
But when the sun starts to fade
Oh she is not a pretty sight.
She trips off her gown of snowflakes
She puts on her muddy jeans
And you cannot see any white!

Mariella Reason (10)
St Louis Catholic Middle School, Bury St Edmunds

The Snow

Snow is a fluffy blanket covering the ice-cold ground
It is a ball of cushion-stuffing
Snow is shredded paper falling from the sky
It is icing sugar on a white, cold cake.

Snow is a giant ice cube
Shattered to a million pieces
Shining silver glitter
Gliding gently from the sky.

Snow is a shower of sparkling diamonds
Angel tears floating down from Heaven
Landing silently like tiny feathers
Making a soft quilt for Mother Nature.

Georgia Burley (10)
St Louis Catholic Middle School, Bury St Edmunds

How Ferret Forms

The brightest star there that night
Would form a ferret in the night,
So as she crept
As she wept
As she stole the grey hair
From the granny's chair
For her fur she stole an arty smarty
And ate and ate till poor magic smarty
Was gone, so in a puff she had some fur.
For her teeth she stole four pieces of glass
From the science class.
She took a shiny bead
For each eye indeed
And for her tongue
Everything went wrong
So poor old ferret could not talk
But only walk.

Rachele Ober (11)
St Louis Catholic Middle School, Bury St Edmunds

Snow Is Alive

Snow is alive with playfulness
It is welcoming but stlll neglected.
Snow is as soft as cotton wool
And it is still powerless.
Snow can wrap around my feet
And although cold, it is still cosy.
Snow has a strong mind
Daydreaming,
Drifting
Snow appears as calm and gentle
But can sometimes be unsettling.
All in all snow is a very strange person
With many varying moods.

Jason Heffron (11)
St Louis Catholic Middle School, Bury St Edmunds

Ice Is . . .

A frightened penguin's lair,
A cold damp nightmare,
The cubes in your drink on a hot summer's day,
An igloo,
The monster that eats your feet,
The eyes that watch you on a cold winter's day,
The shivers down your spine,
The death of an innocent spider,
As white as white as white can be,
Waters best friend,
The walls in the home of its occupant's death,
The teeth of a sabre-toothed tiger,
The thing on your windows when it is cold,
The crunch under your feet in midwinter
And Father Christmas's good luck charm.

Evie Marlow (10)
St Louis Catholic Middle School, Bury St Edmunds

Autumn Leaves

Leaves are a never-ending crunchy carpet everyone wants to buy.
Leaves are very delicate fossils held in a field museum.
They are mini helicopters crashing down to the ground.
They are red arrowheads which keep failing to hit any human passing by.
They are curly cornflakes with rain as their milk.

Max Horkan (9)
St Louis Catholic Middle School, Bury St Edmunds

Autumn Leaves - Haiku

Leaves glide slowly down
Lie softly on the hard ground
Crunching underfoot.

Matthew Chiang (9)
St Louis Catholic Middle School, Bury St Edmunds

Horse Began

(Based on 'Cat Began' by Andrew Matthews)

For her tail
She took the strings of a violin,
She took the swishing of a willow tree's branches
And from a bird's nest she took the weight of a feather.

She seized the speed of a gale,
She stole the strength of ten men,
She took the endurance of a wild river heading towards the sea
And made her motion.

To create her beauty
She took the fur of a silky guinea pig,
She stole the point of a blowing horn for her ears
And for her eyes she took the darkness of midnight.

She grabbed the shine of four bright stars,
She took the darkness of a black diamond,
She stole the firmness of a flint
And make her hooves.
The mane of a lion and the softness of a bunny went into her
own mane
And Horse was created.

Molly O'Donnell (11)
St Louis Catholic Middle School, Bury St Edmunds

What Is The Sun?

The sun is a bright orange beach ball thrown into the beautiful
blue sky,
It is a gold coin placed perfectly on the pale Pacific Ocean.
The sun is a pumpkin on fire, it burns ballistically quick.
The sun's heat is a huge pot of English mustard being poured
on the shimmering sky.
The sun is the inside of the lantern on fire with flickering candle flames.
The sun blazes brightly on the sandy seaside.
The sun is a hot chilli, be careful or it will burn.
The sun is an orange lifeboat floating freely on a brilliant blue sea.

Nicholas Bigg (10)
St Louis Catholic Middle School, Bury St Edmunds

Snake

(Based on 'Cat Began' by Andrew Matthews)

To make snake
It took the roundness of a one pound coin,
It took the blackness of coal,
It took the size of a ping-pong ball
And those were the eyes.

It took the solidness of diamonds,
It took the sharpness of knives,
It took the colour of new snow
And those were the fangs.

It took the sliminess of custard,
It took the sleekness of coins,
It took the shine of a suit of armour
And those were the scales.

It took the shape of a pitchfork,
It took the colour of salmon,
It took the flecks of a moon,
That was the forked tongue.
Then Snake was made.

Auberon Limmer (11)
St Louis Catholic Middle School, Bury St Edmunds

Autumn Leaves

Leaves are a chestnut horse galloping in the moon,
Light with burgundy eyes and a beige mane and tail
It rears on its brown hooves glistening
It swoops down with the wind in its ears
With its graceful movement as it sways in the wind
When I go crunching through my leaves
This is what my imagination tells me.

Jack Fenn (9)
St Louis Catholic Middle School, Bury St Edmunds

The Parrot

(Based on 'Cat Began' by Andrew Matthews)

For his feathers
He took the colours of the rainbow,
He took the brightness of the sun,
He took the softness of the snow.

For his beak
He took the sharpness of the sword,
He took the shine of the stars,
He took the words of a human.

For his claws
He took the shape of the moon's shadow,
He took the sharpness of a needle,
He took the strength of an elephant.

For his eyes
He took the shape of a football,
He took the movement of a pivoting netball player,
He took the darkness of a blackberry
And Parrot was made.

Dominic Turner (10)
St Louis Catholic Middle School, Bury St Edmunds

The Moon Is . . .

A ball of cheese nibbled by mice,
A playground where vampires and werewolves play,
A gigantic boat where witches and wizards have their flying lessons,
A mirror for the sun to shine in all its greatness,
A caring mother for all her baby meteorites,
A hero to Neil Armstrong,
A bowling ball floating in outer space,
A good friend to owls who often visit.

Rachel Sims (10)
St Louis Catholic Middle School, Bury St Edmunds

Snow

Snow
Soft but crispy.
Snow is an abstract
Sifting to the ground.

Sherbets on my mouth
Sizzling on my tongue.
Diamonds and pearls are falling
Gently to the ground.

Snow are crunching
Like a white wolf.
Snow is a feather
Dancing to the ground.

Snow may be heavy
Tough and strong
But snow is ashes
Burnt to the ground.

Thien Nguyen (10)
St Louis Catholic Middle School, Bury St Edmunds

My Favourite Food

It's thick, creamy, luscious and smooth
Do you think it's my favourite food?

You can get it in all shapes and sizes
Large and small, dark and light
Eat it anytime, day or night

It feels so nice in my mouth
I feel as if I want to shout

Now what do you think that it might be
No more clues, it's too easy
Alright, I'll tell you if I must
Or else I fear I'm going to bust
It's . . . chocolate!

Rebecca Hunt (10)
St Louis Catholic Middle School, Bury St Edmunds

My House

My house is always manic,
Dad thinks he's supersonic.
With a tablecloth cape,
Stuck to him with tape,
And a colander for a hat.

My house is so bizarre,
Mum really loves her car.
Round the block all day,
Then down the one way
Where she finally comes to a halt.

My house is always mad,
My brother's mostly bad.
Detention at school,
Just thinking he's cool,
Sticking chewing gum under the desks.

My house is always weird,
My sister's always feared.
With a ginger afro,
And a nose like a crow,
Also failing the beauty contest.

My house is so confusing,
The dog is so refusing.
To stay behind the bar,
Not running afar,
To another town or village.

There's a summary of my family,
Did I forget to mention?
All the neighbours moved out,
I say without a doubt
It was because of my family's reputation.

Eleanor Cockman (10)
St Louis Catholic Middle School, Bury St Edmunds

A Snowy Night

Today I walked with just a little frost
Later on it grew so dark I could not find my door.
I thought I must be last
I finally found it and went inside and saw a snow-covered floor.
I said, 'Is it really that cold?'
Then all of a sudden I felt a chill
It felt like the sun had been sold
Or maybe it was because I lived on top of a hill.

The snow pulled at my feet
While the wind brushed my hair,
I heard my white heartbeat
And I thought I saw a polar bear.

My body was full of goosebumps
From head to toe
Was something playing tricks on my eyes
Yes, it was just the snow
The snow always lies!

Ellie Field (10)
St Louis Catholic Middle School, Bury St Edmunds

Fireworks

I love to see fireworks
They make me stare in wonder
Some of them are really loud
Almost like thunder!

I really like the shapes they make
Especially the stars,
I wonder how far up they go
Maybe even to Mars!

I love the fantastic colours
Red, silver and green,
I can't believe how bright they are
They're the best I've ever seen!

Daniel Howe (10)
St Louis Catholic Middle School, Bury St Edmunds

Wind

The wind is uncontrollably clumsy
With an unpredictable mood
Arms flailing without respect
Rushing here and there, not knowing what to do
Where to go
When to go
He is a gorilla throwing broken branches.

The wind terrorises the people
With energetic speed
Running up the street
Knocking over bins
Pulling down the washing line
It is a lion, uncaring
It sprints to the next village with destruction in its wake.

Joshua Bryan (10)
St Louis Catholic Middle School, Bury St Edmunds

Thunder & Lightning

Dark billowing clouds, a low distant growl
The cats run for cover
The dog starts to howl
A peal of thunder, a streak of lightning
Small children find this truly frightening.

The thunder rolls and crashes around
The lightning zigzags down to the ground,
For a short time there is no noise
The garden is littered with abandoned toys.

Rumble and roar, flash and flicker
Girls and boys start to bicker.
Power lines down, trees burnt to a cinder
I am watching the storm through my window.

Laura Butcher (10)
St Louis Catholic Middle School, Bury St Edmunds

The Sun

The sun is a two-faced menace.
He is like a yellow god
He is an old, wise man
He's the red devil who dries out the land.

He's knowledgeable but sneaky,
He's powerful but quiet.
The heat is warming,
His sunlight badly burns the backs of the innocent.

The menace gives no water
No warning of drought.
He is a ripe banana
But he has no taste.

He gives us light at day and is gone by night
He comes upon the horizon and sunrise is upon us.

Samuel Townsend (10)
St Louis Catholic Middle School, Bury St Edmunds

Hail The Hail

Hail is a robber, an escaped convict and a bully,
Throwing knives at people as it storms around in fury.
To get people out of its way it chops away at their faces.

Crash!
Bang!
Smash!

Faster, forthgoing,
Not caring what it does
Foraging from above.
Searching for something, something, something
What that something is we shall never know.
But that goes to show
Through hail and snow
Hail is like a thief.

Elizabeth Jessop (10)
St Louis Catholic Middle School, Bury St Edmunds

My Weather Poem

I am the whooshing wind
I can be as warm as a fire
Or I can be as cold as ice
But I am not usually seen.

I am the raging rain
I can help the farmers
But I do get people as wet as a river
People will lick from me.

I am the striking storm
I sometimes hurt people
And I am as loud as a lion's roar
People are scared of me

I am the furious fog
And I look big and fierce
People get stuck in my black
But I don't hurt anyone.

Henley Kennedy (10)
St Louis Catholic Middle School, Bury St Edmunds

Lightning

Zigzag flashes of lightning cut across the sky
Just as well it's way up high.
Bolts that jump from cloud to cloud
Followed by a thunderous sound.
Lighting seeks out its prey,
Will you live to fight another day?
Lightning is faster than the speed of sound,
Anything quicker can't be found.
Lightning lights up the clouds at night
So you don't have to switch on the light.
Hotter than the sun, it would incinerate a nun!

Daniel Kingsbury (10)
St Louis Catholic Middle School, Bury St Edmunds

The Storm

When a storm begins to build
The pressure is intense
From the lightest rustling of the leaves
To the rattling of the fence.

The skies begin to darken
Pitter-patter goes the rain
The loudest crack of thunder
Water rushing down the drain.

The wind is really howling
Lightning fills the skies
The storm is really at its peak
I can't believe my eyes.

Things are slowly calming
I see a sunshine ray
The storm has gone away now
To return another day.

Joe Arthurs (10)
St Louis Catholic Middle School, Bury St Edmunds

Frost

Frost is hard and cold and cruel
He sweeps across the midnight sky
Leaving a shimmering trail in his wake.

All through the night Frost works away
Gliding over city and forest alike
Hiding away from the sun.

His trail crunches loudly as you step on it
It cracks and splinters
Into millions of tiny pieces.

Hannah Dance (10)
St Louis Catholic Middle School, Bury St Edmunds

Snow

Snow.
The snow is a lonely friend
Always there to play.
He is welcoming to children
As he floats to the ground.
He's happy to help a child
Laying all the time.
Snowball fights,
Snowmen,
Snow angels.
Soft as a blanket,
Crunchy as ice
White as a sheet of paper.
As night falls it sits alone
Without a friend to talk to.
Snow.

Darcie Cowap (10)
St Louis Catholic Middle School, Bury St Edmunds

Matthew Hunter

The lights turn to life
Cars turn to rats
Generators growl
And headlamps glare.

Buildings overlook houses
Bikes squeak
Fans howl
Gutters gulp.

People-like statues stare
Pollution haunts the nostrils
Shadows come to life and
Window-like eyes follow you.

Matthew Hunter (11)
St Louis Catholic Middle School, Bury St Edmunds

Frost

He sleeps in the day, comes out at night
A heart as cold as ice, as sly as a fox he climbs up walls,
Roams the streets leaving his glittering silver trail wherever he goes.
He turns grass into tiny blades of ice covering his wonderful
midnight kingdom
In an almost magical blanket of white.
From street to street he travels leaving no trace but his wonderful trail.
He stares through steamed-over windows leaving his icy fingerprints
all over them.
But as the sun slowly creeps over the horizon Frost grows weaker,
weaker and weaker.
As he melts into the ground, Frost loses his wonderful shimmer
and his magical glittery coating
By noon, Frost is no more.

James Nixon (11)
St Louis Catholic Middle School, Bury St Edmunds

Autumn

As I took my first step into autumn
The world turned yellow ochre
The trees were desert-yellow
The copper leaves were as brown as rusty metal.

As the falling chocolate-brown conkers rested on the ground
A murky mist fell over the land
My body was filled with the crisp feeling of autumn
It was like living in a world of foggy nothingness.

The crackling noises were making my ears tingle
But the beige world was coming to an end
The autumn colours were fading away
Then white fell from the sky.

Guy Beetham (9)
St Louis Catholic Middle School, Bury St Edmunds

Crocodile Began

(Based on 'Cat Began' by Andrew Matthews)

For his eyes
He took the colour from an emerald,
He took the shape from a shining marble,
His eyes were made.

For his teeth
He took the edge of a silver saw,
He took the power from a bolt of lightning,
His teeth were made.

For his back
He took the roughness of bark,
He took the uneven points from flints,
His back was made.

For his feet
He took the shape of a spade,
He took the shards of glass for claws,
His feet were made.

For his tail
He took the crack of a whip,
He took the strike of a snake,
The crocodile was made.

Emma Healey (10)
St Louis Catholic Middle School, Bury St Edmunds

The Stars That Shine

The stars that shine in the night as bright as the sun of the day
They sparkle like glitter, a pretty sight to see.
The stars, the moon, the black night, the mist, the owl,
A little boy that never sleeps.
No birds, no children laughing, just black, the silent sound of night.
The stars are angels, men and women that died have a second life.

George Lester (10)
St Louis Catholic Middle School, Bury St Edmunds

Penguin Began

(Based on 'Cat Began' by Andrew Matthews)

Penguin began.
He took the silk from a silk farm,
He stole the black and white from an old film
And made his body.

For his beak
He grabbed the yellow from a banana,
He took the curve from a curvy sword,
He took the thickness from oak to make his beak.

For his feet,
He stole the orange from the sunset,
He took the web from a duck
And that made his feet.

For his movement
He took the waddle from a fat human,
He stole the slide from a dry ski slope
And that made his movement.

For his eyes
He got the sharpness from an owl,
He got the roundness from marbles
And that made Penguin.

Sebastian Lawson (10)
St Louis Catholic Middle School, Bury St Edmunds

Autumn Leaves

Leaves are diamonds, rubies and emeralds on a gold necklace.
Leaves are the sparks of burning fire, orange, scarlet, red and yellow.
Leaves are a chocolate bar just made; it smells delicious
in the autumn.
Leaves are parts of beautiful butterflies, red, orange, yellow and green.
Leaves are the stars in the sky, gold and yellow on a dark black tree.

Renee Zdrenka (10)
St Louis Catholic Middle School, Bury St Edmunds

How Flying Turtle Began

(Based on 'Cat Began' by Andrew Matthews)

He took the boulders on a hill,
He took iron from the centre of the Earth,
He took the sun's heat and made his shell.

For his legs
He took the colour of grass,
He took the dinosaur's teeth,
He took the scales of a green snake.

He took the scales of a dragon,
He took the hugeness of a dragon's wings,
He took the colour of the sea for his wings.

For his head
He took the colour of an iron plate,
He took the fire from a dragon's throat
And Flying Turtle was made.

Danny Pym-Hember (10)
St Louis Catholic Middle School, Bury St Edmunds

Autumn

Autumn leaves falling down,
Red, yellow, golden brown.
Squirrels collecting nuts for winter,
Hedgehogs snuffling, seeking shelter.
Nights get longer, days get shorter,
Soon I'll need my woolly jumper.
Pumpkins ripening, for Hallowe'en,
Trick or treat? Don't be mean!
Autumn's damp with misty mornings,
Summer's gone but Christmas is coming.

Joe Burrell (9)
St Louis Catholic Middle School, Bury St Edmunds

Snow

The snow is a daydream girl
She is welcoming to everyone
And eager to have some friends
Kind and gentle
She is very playful.

But she is unreliable
Coming and going throughout the winter
Powerless and neglected
Calling for friends through the night
Indecisive, unsettling.

Hard and icy, yet she can be
Jolly, cosy and playful
Waiting and waiting
For someone to play with her
Drifting about in her snowy blanket
Leaving a snowy path behind her.

Claudia Codling (10)
St Louis Catholic Middle School, Bury St Edmunds

The Leopard

I saw a leopard jump in the air
I saw it catch a golden hare
I saw it with its golden fur
I saw it on a rock doing a purr

I saw it in a desert bare
Running faster than a flare
All the trees were now dead
All the elephants were in bed.

I saw it eating all the deer
All were running with fear
Far away there was a herd
Circled by a purple bird.

Freddie McKendrick (9)
St Louis Catholic Middle School, Bury St Edmunds

Wind

The wind is a clumsy energetic force
In a happy but lonely way
He whistles along very sad
Taking everything in his path
Taking branches and twigs
Taking people's belongings
Leaving nothing behind.

He is alone, expressing his anger
Wind is an uncontrollable youth
Nothing gets in his way
He becomes a vicious vandal
Creating ultimate destruction
After his horrible temper
He becomes quiet and cool
Just a delicate breeze.

Simon Codling (10)
St Louis Catholic Middle School, Bury St Edmunds

Moving To A New House

We're moving to this funny old house
It's gloomy and grey inside.
But they're packing boxes anyway
There is nowhere left to hide.

They say, 'Come on, we have got to go
And you have just got to come.'
Even the dog is now in the car
There is nowhere left to run.

It turns out that it is not too bad
But I'm still filled with sorrow
At the loss of my comforting house
And rabbits with their burrows.

Emilia Jewell (9)
St Louis Catholic Middle School, Bury St Edmunds

Frost

Frost is a cold-hearted bully
Who sneaks around at night.
As he walks everything around him
Is covered in a shimmering shine.

Frost sweeps up the walls
Leaving a crunching blanket behind him.
Every crack is filled with white dust
As he shakes it off himself carelessly.

Frost is spiteful
Because everyone shivers at his presence.
Frost is bitter and vain
He likes tripping people for no reason.

Frost sends a tingle down my back
Forcing me to wrap up warmly.
He wants to remind me
He is always following me.

Frost never gives in
He is tough, icy cold and
Doesn't have a care
But is quick and sharp as well.

Frost is like a midnight monster
Out at night,
Gone by day
But always leaving his frosty mark.

Although Frost is bitter,
Vain, sharp,
There is one thing that terrifies him . . .
Sunrise!

Aimee Moore (11)
St Louis Catholic Middle School, Bury St Edmunds

About A Hippo

About a hippo
You should know
You wouldn't like him
On your toe.

He's just as heavy
As a house
His ears are tiny
Like a mouse.

He loves to wallow
Like a pig
His chunky feet
Are way too big!

With gappy teeth
And smelly breath
This clumsy oaf
Could crush you to death.

If in Africa
Watch where you go
Be sure to avoid
An ugly hippo!

Ellie Brierley (10)
St Louis Catholic Middle School, Bury St Edmunds

The River Of Love

Love is like a flowing river
Up and down it goes
Zooming fast
As it travels past
The bend.

Romana Cassinelli (10)
St Louis Catholic Middle School, Bury St Edmunds

Bushbaby Began

(Based on 'Cat Began' by Andrew Matthews)

For his tail
He took a piece of fluffy silk
He took the softness of the sand of Cromer beach
And made his tail.

For his feet
He took the leather of the cow
He stole the wool from the shop in town
And made his feet.

For his nose
He took the blackness of the night
He took a lovely jet stone from the sea
And made his nose.

For his ears
He took the sense of a shark
He took the ears of a dog
And the bushbaby was made.

Liam Gladden (10)
St Louis Catholic Middle School, Bury St Edmunds

Shadows

Black as night, strange as mist
Fading as the evening nears
Stalking men and women too
Treading steps that no one hears.

In the dark they are not here
Turn on a torch and they appear
Eating, playing, cooking too
They will copy all you do.

If you walk right out to sea
That is where it will be
Silent, creeping friend or foe
Which one are you? I'll never know.

Isobel Broughton (9)
St Louis Catholic Middle School, Bury St Edmunds

My Sisters

My sisters are the golden sun
My sisters are full of fun
My sisters are the bright blue sky
My sisters are the apples of my eye

Molly is the first little dude
Molly loves to eat her food
Molly loves to lark about
Molly loves to scream and shout

Lily is number two
Lily likes to stick and glue
Lily likes to run and run
Lily, Lily is lots of fun.

My sisters are like a ray of light
My sisters set my heart alight
My sisters are like the wild sea
My sisters mean the world to me.

Joshua Ellis (9)
St Louis Catholic Middle School, Bury St Edmunds

A Friend

A friend is someone who understands
And is patient,
Someone you can trust
With friendship.

A friend is more than a friend
It's love,
A friend you know well
Wise and brave.

A friend is noble
And kind,
Comforting and secret,

A friend is a dog.

Hannah Griffiths (9)
St Louis Catholic Middle School, Bury St Edmunds

They're Always Making Trouble

I saw four people playing in the leaves
Messing up all the place
I don't know what to do
Now I'm starting to pace.

I saw four people throwing snow at
Everybody around
I don't know what to do
They're making a load of sound.

I saw four people throwing water
At everyone's windows and doors
I don't know what to do
They should be down at the shores.

I saw four people
Wrecking all the flowers
When they could have some proper fun
Playing by the towers.

I finally saw four people
Playing kindly in their house
They have found something to do
They're quiet as a mouse.

Tyrone Alleyne (10)
St Louis Catholic Middle School, Bury St Edmunds

Midge, My Border Collie

She dashes through the fields
The rabbit is her prey
She runs through the forest
And comes back at dawn of day.

Emily Wallace (9)
St Louis Catholic Middle School, Bury St Edmunds

School

My friends Ciara, Lucy, Honor
Annoying people, Daniel, William, Connor.
Great teachers, Mr and Mrs Kirk, also Mrs G
All in a school to explore and see.

Rhyming couplets are boring
I'd rather do drawing
But reading is fun
Though sometimes I wish all my work was done.

Gazing out the window at the hot sun
As all the children play and run
In PE we're doing gymnastics
In games, netball practise.

On the bus
No nonsense, no fuss
Relating sudden images of Mr and Mrs Kirk
Shouting, 'Do your homework!'

Amelia Nunn (9)
St Louis Catholic Middle School, Bury St Edmunds

The Snake

(Based on 'Cat Began' by Andrew Matthews)

For its teeth it took the yellow from the sand,
The brightness from the blazing sun
And it took the sharpness from some daggers
And its teeth were made.
For its scales it took the green from the leaves
The roughness of some rocky gravel
And it took the shine from the moon
And its scales were made.
For its eyes it took the sparkle from the stars,
The dazzling dew from the grass
And its pupil is as dark as a beetle
And the snake was made.

Jack Arnold (11)
St Louis Catholic Middle School, Bury St Edmunds

The Element Of Surprise

Walking on your own
Finding your way home
Don't make one squeaky little sound
Or you just might be found

Then something touches you
It makes you jump
Your heart goes thump
You can't say anything.

Funny tummy
Wanting your mummy.

You're completely numb
Aching limbs
You're all so stunned
Hurting inside
Nowhere to hide.

That is the unpleasant
Element of surprise.

Emily Bromham (10)
St Louis Catholic Middle School, Bury St Edmunds

The Leaves Are As . . .

The leaves are . . .
As yellow as a melon,
As green as grass,
As orange as the sun,
As brown as chocolate,
As red as a ruby,
As golden as a trophy,
As pale as your skin,
As beige as a biscuit,
As bronze as a sunset and
As rusty as a nail.

Georgie Fish (9)
St Louis Catholic Middle School, Bury St Edmunds

A Bear

There is a cuddly toy
On a chair,
He rises in the sky,
He is a loving bear.
There are all types of bears
But this one is red,
This one is nice and cuddly
You could sleep with him in your bed.
This bear is very small
And he makes new friends,
My bear's name is Conor
And his love he sends.
He likes playing football
He lives in Bury
He is a good sport
And it makes him merry.

Benedict Browning (9)
St Louis Catholic Middle School, Bury St Edmunds

Autumn Leaves

Leaves are fireworks
With beautiful colours.

Leaves are red rubies
Shining in the sun.

Leaves are exotic birds
With multicoloured feathers.

Leaves are arrowheads
Flying in the sky.

Leaves are lizards
Camouflaged in the trees.

Leaves are helicopters
Coming in to land.

Niamh O'Donoghue (9)
St Louis Catholic Middle School, Bury St Edmunds

Autumn

Autumn is upon us
The leaves are going brown,
The sky is turning misty and
Conkers are falling down.

Hallowe'en is coming,
Pumpkins fill the street.
Evening's get darker
As we all go trick or treat.

Bonfire Night is near,
The fireworks sparkle in the sky.
A crackling burning bonfire,
The flames are like arms reaching high.

Autumn is coming to an end
Winter will be here soon.
The dark winter clouds are blowing
Next to the big yellow moon.

Emily Ritchie (9)
St Louis Catholic Middle School, Bury St Edmunds

Autumn

Autumn leaves falling down
On the trees and on the ground
Colours, yellows, browns and reds
Somersault around my head.

Early frost makes leaves all brown
Summer over, falling down
As I kick crisp leaves aside
Summer memories will abide.

Autumn comes upon a pace
Winter warmth shall me embrace
Until the spring shall bring anew
Fresh green leaves and morning dew.

Emily Eustace (9)
St Louis Catholic Middle School, Bury St Edmunds

What Happens In Autumn

Autumn comes once a year
Autumn breeze blows through my ear
Autumn trees turn bright gold
Autumn leaves do not hold.

As the day becomes much shorter
Hallowe'en can scare your daughter
Orange pumpkins start to swell
Scary stories there are to tell.

Trick or treat in the street
Lots of sweets for us to eat
Celebrating the harvest festival
Gathering in all the fruit and vegetables.

Collecting wood for Bonfire Night
Sparklers glow really bright.
Shiny conkers fall to the ground
Waiting there to be found.

The trees in the parks turn to sticks
All the gold and brown leaves start to mix.
Everybody knows that winter is so very near
But I still think autumn is the best time of the year.

Billy Spillane (9)
St Louis Catholic Middle School, Bury St Edmunds

My Family

M ummy loves me very much
Y esterday she kissed me

F amilies stick together
A nd my daddy loves me too
M y cousins like playing with me
I n my house we live together with my dog Rhum
L ove all around me
Y our family is the most special thing ever.

Hannah McAuley (9)
St Louis Catholic Middle School, Bury St Edmunds

My Own World

Different coloured flowers
Here and there,
Are pieces of all different paintings
As thin as a hair.

Roses on a rose bush
Are fingers chopped off by the gods,
Telling all people who do not forgive
That they are as worthless as cods.

Scared little hedgehogs
Are like a big bundle of knives,
Telling you, do not harm them
But almost nothing cares for their lives.

The everlasting sky
A giant sea of wonder,
Sheltering another world
And on it we may ponder.

The glistening, colourful, bright fish
In the deep, royal blue sea.
A reflection of the giant pond above us
Is what it is said to be.

The sound of the roaring, angry thunder
In the dark, navy blue sky
Is Jesus scolding the people who have done wrong
And teaching them never to lie.

His death, resurrection and new name to glory
Teaches us all to be good in our lives
To follow in His name and listen to His stories
And hope that here, He once again arrives.

Grace Sinnott (9)
St Louis Catholic Middle School, Bury St Edmunds

Autumn Day

The trees are ablaze
Copper sparks in the air
Mountain of leaves
Someone follows their path.

The foggy air
Damp green grass
The mushrooms are in the air
Now comes the sound of the hares.

Out comes the sun
Kids play in the woods
People try to catch the leaves
You hear the laughter from the fun.

Now the sun tries to hide in the trees
The sky goes purple
As it goes dark.

Out comes the moon, a big round ball
It gives the sky a big white glow.

Clement Ehall (9)
St Louis Catholic Middle School, Bury St Edmunds

Autumn

A utumn is here
U nusual colours around
T rees go empty
U nderneath my feet you hear crunchy sounds
M ore animals disappear
N o more summer for a year

I look around so many things to see
S o many changes staring at me

H iding in the woods under leaves and almost everything
E ars are listening out for
R abbits and squirrels asleep until spring
E yes wide open for a new season to begin.

Sydney Maguire (9)
St Louis Catholic Middle School, Bury St Edmunds

Swimming

I love swimming in a pool or the sea,
It's always such fun and as cool as can be.
I love to splash; it's great to dive,
I always feel so happy and alive!

When the freezing cold sea touches my boiling face,
I'm as happy as a bird in my rightful place.
My dog swims with me in that searing, icy sea,
The pair of us together as content as can be!

I swim in the pool with my family
And we're all as happy and healthy as you can see.
I love doing backstroke, front crawl and sitting dives,
I like doing somersaults and feeling great and alive.

The salty taste of the water stings my lips,
It makes me want to do a flip!
I'd enjoy swimming with dolphins and tropical fish,
I'd love to dive for treasure, it's my greatest wish.

When I swim I feel fantastic, fabulous and fit,
It's like writing a story but with an extra kick!
Now it's time to leave the pool, to get out and get changed,
But I'll start swimming soon again, some sunny, bright day.

Eleanor Kitching (10)
St Louis Catholic Middle School, Bury St Edmunds

What Animal Am I?

I am a meat eater
I am a zebra but with black and orange lines
I am a smelly animal
I am not a pet
I am an enlarged cat
I am a crafty animal
I am a tiger.

Eleanor Skittrall (9)
St Louis Catholic Middle School, Bury St Edmunds

The Roar Of The Wind, The Anger Of The Sea

The roar of the wind, the anger of the sea
Combined are indestructible.
Together they sunk the unsinkable,
Their almighty strength unpredictable but ruling.

Screams were heard within her bowels
But the sea and the wind had no mercy.
They are in control, not a colossal ship
Which compared to them was weak.

The roar of the wind, the anger of the sea
Respect nothing of the boats, ships or swimmers
In the sea, tossing them around
Helpless and lifeless.

The sea will rise above you,
The wind will work against you,
To summon forth a tempest.
Together the wind and sea are indestructible.

Xara Thomas-Morrill (9)
St Louis Catholic Middle School, Bury St Edmunds

Hummingbird

Hummingbirds flapping their wings so fast
You can hear them humming as they fly past.
Flapping fast through the trees
Faster than the bumblebees.
Lots are flying here and there
Hummingbirds are everywhere.
There's a few flying over that cloud
They all look ever so proud.
A tiny bird with so much power
Taking nectar from every flower.
I could watch them all for hours
Popping in and out of the bright flowers.

Molly Russell (9)
St Louis Catholic Middle School, Bury St Edmunds

Finding Bonnie, My Dog

Come back from Wood Green
Dad on the computer,
'Come and look at this one
A black Labrador, Bonnie, just in.'

RSPCA, miles away
Dogs in cages, find her at last.
Growling, barking, leaping
Then sniffing, looking hopeful.

Bringing her home, Mum and me,
A walking spider, legs everywhere.
At home, sniffing, running, searching,
Finding her bed, settling in.

Dog's holiday, backing away
From the waves,
Drinking saltwater, running on the sand,
Playing fetch with stones.

Bonnie the thief, gate left open
Takes her chance,
Devastation of Easter eggs,
Leaving me writhing with anger!

Coming home to Bonnie,
Gift of a toy, wet nose
Whole body wagging,
Wailing with excitement.

Bonnie, black seal head,
Ears like flags, soft as silk,
Glistening black, long lashes
Melting chocolate eyes.

Bethan Gent (9)
St Louis Catholic Middle School, Bury St Edmunds

Red, Orange And Green

Red
Red is a bright apple washing under a tap,
Red X marks the spot on a treasure map.
Red is the colour of anger and fear,
There is such a thing as a little red deer.
Red is the colour of a dew-dropped rose,
Red is the colour of my garden hose.
Red is the colour of a kitchen mop,
Red is the colour of boiling hot.

Orange
Orange is a bowl of honey as sticky as can be,
Orange is a bumblebee passing to see what he can see.
Orange is a sun burning in the sky,
Orange is a bird gently flying by.
Orange is a tomcat sitting on the wall,
Orange is a raisin cake waiting on a stall.
Orange is my orange sock,
Orange is my front door if only you would knock.

Green
Green is freshly cut grass,
Beer bottles have green glass.
New leaves with a fresh smell,
The green moss around an old well.
Green is the colour of our kettle,
Green is the colour of a stinging nettle.
Green is the colour of a field of new wheat,
Green is the colour of infected feet.

Ciara O'Donnell (9)
St Louis Catholic Middle School, Bury St Edmunds

My Family

Dad is the strongest,
He is in charge of all the tools.
He eats the most at meal times
And makes up all the rules.

Mum can be a grump,
But I know that she loves me.
She is very good and kind
And makes wonderful tea.

Laura is the pretty one,
She is as sweet as toffee.
She uses lots of lipstick
And takes me out for coffee.

Joe is the funny one,
He likes to play a joke.
He is friendly and funny
And gets on with all sorts of folk.

Tom is the clever one,
He really likes history.
He is always very happy
And likes a book with a mystery.

Alice is so sporty,
She also likes to dance.
She could probably win the X Factor
Given half a chance.

Lucy is the youngest,
Though she makes a lot of noise.
She makes a mess of all the rooms
Covering them with toys.

There is someone I've forgotten,
I wonder who it could be.
Of course, I've just remembered,
The most important person, *me!*

Emily Markham (9)
St Louis Catholic Middle School, Bury St Edmunds

Oryx Was Made

(Based on 'Cat Began' by Andrew Matthews)

Oryx began.
He stole the sharpness of a thorn,
The sleekness of a smooth car bonnet
And made his majestic horns.

He took the fear of a shrew,
The self preservation of a cat
And made his shyness.

For his speed and agility
He pilfered the legs and feet of an Olympic athlete
And seized the power of a Ferrari.

He snatched the darkness of pitch
And the brown of rich mud
And made his furry coat.

He stole the softness of heather
And the straightness of hay
And his mane was made.

And so Oryx was created.

Andrew Williams (10)
St Louis Catholic Middle School, Bury St Edmunds

My Dog

My dog is a zip of lightning running towards me.
He has a coat of golden silk,
He is so cute,
He has a chest of white, white milk.

If he were an aeroplane his ears would be his wings.
He has eyes of dark, dark wood,
Like the singing wind he howls.

I love him very, very much,
I am amazed at how soft he is every time I touch him.

Niamh Lundy (9)
St Louis Catholic Middle School, Bury St Edmunds

Penguin Began

(Based on 'Cat Began' by Andrew Matthews)

Penguin began.

For her coat she took the feathers of a swan
And the softness of a pillow.
Her coat was like a fluff ball,
Her coat was made.

For her eyes she took darkness from night
And the sparkle from the stars.
Her eyes were like sapphires,
Her eyes were made.

For her feet she took the rubber from a tyre
And the colour from the autumn leaves.
Her feet were like rubber,
Her feet were made.

Then . . . Penguin was made.

Megan Iron & Ellen Goodall (11)
St Louis Catholic Middle School, Bury St Edmunds

Parrot Began

(Based on 'Cat Began' by Andrew Matthews)

Parrot began . . .

He took the voice of an annoying girl,
He took the tongue of a lizard,
He stole some buttons off a jacket
And made the face.

He stole the colours from the rainbow,
He took the feathers from a goose,
He took the wings from an eagle
That made the body.

He took the twigs from a tree,
This grew into legs and feet.
He grew claws to hang onto branches
And that made a parrot.

Andrew Wilson (10)
St Louis Catholic Middle School, Bury St Edmunds

Wolf Began

(Based on 'Cat Began' by Andrew Matthews)

Wolf began.
He took the loudness of a church bell,
He took the screeching of a rusty door hinge
For his deafening howl.

He took the bristles from a broom,
He took the long curve of a sickle
For his bushy tail.

He took the silence of landing snow,
He took the knowledge and speed of a Zulu chief
For his stealth.

He took the sharpness of a knife,
He took the piercing of an arrow through flesh
For his teeth.

He took the hope of an army general,
He took a fragment of the moon in the middle of the night
For his longing eyes
And Wolf was made.

Joe Tasker (10)
St Louis Catholic Middle School, Bury St Edmunds

Frost

Frost is a cold-hearted creature with a mind as sharp as ice.
He creeps through the darkness leaving a shimmering trail covering
the ground with ice.
After his visit the windows are crusted with white,
The ground is so slippery underfoot.
He climbs up the walls after darkness leaving his coating of silver
He's never wandering while the sun is up for if he did he would die.
As you walk over his blanket of ice he leaps up and bites you.
He sneaks through the streets silently, sneakily.

Phoebe Allsopp (10)
St Louis Catholic Middle School, Bury St Edmunds

How Giraffe Began

(Based on 'Cat Began' by Andrew Matthews)

For his tail he stole a hog brush wrapped in the roots of an oak tree
Then added the sparkles of stars for all to see.
Next he thought about his spots.
He took puddles and paled them on him,
After taking bark and covering the puddles
He took shiny gold dyed brown and melted it onto his spots,
They were now spots not dots.

For his tongue he stole the snake's slither
Poured the water out of puddles to make it moist.
He mimicked the caterpillars wrapping so that he could eat
Then he thought hard, next, designing his feet.

Giraffe thought hard and long.
He borrowed the zebra's long legs for himself before stealing
the horse's hooves.
He was proud of his feet so added the weight of a balloon
His legs were beautiful and beamed like the moon.

For his eyes he took a journey to space,
Not a waste of time.
For his eyes he used many colours red and lime.
The sparkles of stars were added
Into these colours he padded
The beauty of the planets
Before returning home to eat some pomegranates.

Daniel Martin (11)
St Louis Catholic Middle School, Bury St Edmunds

The Elephant Began

(Based on 'Cat Began' by Andrew Matthews)

The elephant began
He took the point of a needle,
He stole the curve of a knife
That made the tusk.

He stole the width of a football,
He took the cracks of the savannah floor,
He borrowed the softness of a sponge
And that made the feet.

He took the length of a baby giraffe,
He stole the use of a hose,
He borrowed the movement of a snake
And that made the trunk.

He took the colour of a winter sky,
He stole the texture of a wise man's forehead,
He borrowed the thickness of a baby's arm
And that made the skin.

He stole the thinness of a pancake,
He borrowed the motion of a door,
He took the use of a fan
And that made the ears
And Elephant was made.

Joshua Grover (11)
St Louis Catholic Middle School, Bury St Edmunds

Dog Began

(Based on 'Cat Began' by Andrew Matthews)

Dog began.
He took the whine of an alarm,
He took the growl of an angry lion
And made his voice.

For his speed
He stole a motorbike's engine,
He stole the energy from a speedy cheetah
And made his speed.

For his loyalty
He seized the heart of a faithful servant,
He seized the friendship between two friends
And made his loyalty.

For his teeth
He swiped the sharpness of a dagger,
He swiped the whiteness of snow
And made his teeth.

For his fur
He grasped the smoothness of feathers,
He grasped the warmth of a sweaty sauna
And made his fur

And Dog was made.

Jake Head (11)
St Louis Catholic Middle School, Bury St Edmunds

The Dog Begins

(Based on 'Cat Began' by Andrew Matthews)

Dog begins.
For his voice
He took the fierce howl of a wolf
And the growl of a rumbling car.

For his eyes
He took the shining of stars,
The blackness of coal
And the reflection of the sun.

For his fur
He took the stuffing out of a big pillow
And the feathers of a bird.

For his claws
He stole the sharpness of nails
And the dirtiness of mud.

For his teeth
He stole the whiteness of paper
And the sharpness of a shard of metal

And the dog was made.

Henry White (10)
St Louis Catholic Middle School, Bury St Edmunds

The Frog Story

Once there was a princess
One day she was feeling mad
She yelled at her younger sister
Sometimes she was quite bad.

Then a small parcel arrived in the post
It said Princess Tilly
Tilly scowled at the parcel
Though she knew she was being silly.

Tilly opened the parcel
She hoped it was a dog,
She tore off the wrapping paper
And saw it was a frog.

'What am I supposed to do
With this dreadful thing?
I shall go and tell my parents
The queen and the king.'

Then the princess remembered
In her little sister's book
The lady kissed the frog
'I can't remember what happened next, I'll have to take a look.'

So Tilly kissed the ugly frog
What happened next?
But oh no,
A froggy prince and a froggy princess!

Niamh O'Sullivan (8)
St Margaret's CE (VA) Primary School, Ipswich

Lunchtime

Every day at lunchtime
Samantha the Thin
Will stare and look at the cook
Without a simple grin.

She cries and sucks her thumb
While watching others stuff their faces
She won't eat anything
Not even smiley faces.

The dinner lady's grumpy
And the cook is very sad,
The children are still happy
But all the teachers think she's bad.

At the end of lunchtime
All the adults sigh,
They let her mum pick her up
And she smiles and says bye-bye.

Munashe Chagonda (10)
St Margaret's CE (VA) Primary School, Ipswich

Pirate's Treasure Chest

In the pirate's treasure chest there was . . .
A bright red jewel,
Millions of shiny coins,
A horrible broken crown,
A flat blue football,
Dirty bones
And a disgusting piece of seaweed!

Daniel Wallis (8)
St Mary's CE (VA) Primary School, Mildenhall

Queen's Handbag

In the Queen's handbag there was . . .
A pink shiny amethyst as beautiful as gold,
A blue diamond as blue as the sea,
A shiny crown as shiny as silver,
A soft, cuddly, tortoiseshell kitten called Chelsea,
And some make-up to make the Queen pretty,
A picture of her family to keep memories of them,
Some sweet strawberries, sweeter than any I've seen,
Some mouldy sandwiches as mouldy as old skeletons,
A pink shiny phone to phone her friends,
A red diary to write secrets,
Some prisoners' handcuffs and keys to keep bad people away,
A cuddly puppy to cuddle in bed,
A dirty purple dummy as dirty as mud,
A green purse to keep money in,
A gold watch to tell the time,
A silver pen to write in her diary
And some gold and silver jewellery to make her look beautiful.

Have you got any of the Queen's treasure?

Bethany Rolfe (9)
St Mary's CE (VA) Primary School, Mildenhall

In The Thief's Pocket There Was . . .

In the thief's pocket there was . . .
A wonderful, sparkling, gorgeous coin,
A wonderful, expensive ring,
An old, smelly, ugly, stinky boot,
A smashing, super, fantastic crown,
A lovely, delicious hot dog,
A super, enormous purse,
A smashing and wonderful, splendid MP3 player
And an excellent and superb wand.

Kieran Tuffs (8)
St Mary's CE (VA) Primary School, Mildenhall

Sadness

Sadness sounds like nice, calm music.
Sadness tastes like wet, sloppy tears.
Sadness smells like blossom falling from a tree.
Sadness looks like your red-rose heart breaking.
Sadness feels like a pink rose petal.
Sadness reminds me of smooth sand falling out of my hand.
Sadness feels like a fluffy cloud falling from the sky.
Sadness feels like a smooth apple.
Sadness waits till the end of the month.
Sadness looks like the round white moon.
Sadness is as smooth as the ocean.

Olivia Hinchley (8)
St Mary's CE (VA) Primary School, Mildenhall

Mum's Handbag

In my mum's handbag there is . . .
A red and silver phone,
A purple fluffy diary as secret as the deepest secret,
A pink pen with glitter on it,
Money as shiny as a crystal
And a cupcake with icing and a cherry on the top!

Hannah Jenkins (8)
St Mary's CE (VA) Primary School, Mildenhall

Fear

Fear is like a volcano and like a shark coming towards you.
It tastes like a slug, slimy and gooey.
It feels like a boxer knocking you out.
It reminds me of a builder hammering a nail into a piece of wood.
It sounds like a roaring tiger chasing you.

Swayley Smith (8)
St Mary's CE (VA) Primary School, Mildenhall

Happy

Happy is when you are ringing the bells and listening to the bells.
Happy is when you are going somewhere fun.
Happy is doing stuff.
Happy is when you are playing in the park.
Happy is when you are playing with a cat.
Happy is when you are playing with toys.
Happy is when you like being at school.
Happy is when you like listening to assembly.
Happy is when you like doing maths.
Happy is when you like doing things.

Cameron Paterson (8)
St Mary's CE (VA) Primary School, Mildenhall

Darkness

Darkness looks like the black night
Not a thing to see, not a light, all black.
Darkness smells like a stench from the garbage in a bin for
thousands of years,
Nobody would want to be like that.
Darkness reminds me of hatred, lots and lots of hatred.
Darkness takes away the happiness.

Callum Orford (9)
St Mary's CE (VA) Primary School, Mildenhall

Anger

Anger sounds like you're mad and angry.
Anger sounds scary.
Anger tastes sick and horrified.
Anger smells puke-ish and horrible.
Anger looks wild and twitchery.
Anger feels bad and wrecking.

Jack Marsh (8)
St Mary's CE (VA) Primary School, Mildenhall

Silence

Silence sounds like peeling an orange.
Silence sounds like reading a book silently.
Silence tastes like eating a soft apple.
Silence tastes like eating a bit of soft cream.
Silence smells like a bit of wet paint.
Silence smells like juicy red cherries.
Silence looks like someone sleeping as silent as a bird that's still.
Silence looks like a cloud not talking at all.
Silence feels like nothing in the air.
Silence feels like a smooth bit of silk.
Silence reminds me of when it was all silent in the classroom.
Silence reminds me of a bike going on a smooth path.
Silence reminds me of a trolley on soft floor.
Silence reminds me of a sweet storybook.

Hannah Rolfe (8)
St Mary's CE (VA) Primary School, Mildenhall

In The Pirate's Treasure Chest There Was . . .

In the pirate's treasure chest there was . . .
A donkey that was as fierce as a T-Rex,
An angry octopus,
A cat teddy,
A stinky nappy,
His loving mother,
A football to play with,
A foot spa for swollen feet,
A pink lipstick,
His beautiful wife,
The queen who hates him.

Jamie Morley (8)
St Mary's CE (VA) Primary School, Mildenhall

Love

Love sounds like a calm wind at spring.
Love tastes like lipstick freshly made on Christmas Day.
Love smells like a whole new world.
Love looks neater than the bride and groom on their wedding day.
Love feels like a body's smooth hair.
Love reminds me of silky pyjamas.
Love is a whole new experience.
My life is full of love.
Love is like a rainbow.
Love surrounds my heart.
Love is gold, silver and copper.
When I open a treasure box it is full of love.
Love is as sweet as sugar.
Love is as romantic as a candle.
Love is as peaceful as a rose.
Love is everything that's sweet.
Love is a lovely figure.
Love is confetti.

Jasmin Glavin (8)
St Mary's CE (VA) Primary School, Mildenhall

Love

Love sounds like wedding bells.
Love tastes like Valentine's chocolate.
Love smells like sweets.
Love looks like red hearts.
Love feels like red silk.
Love reminds me of my loving family.

Love sounds like birds singing.
Love tastes like sweet cherries.
Love smells like minty breath.
Love looks like people daydreaming at each other.
Love feels like someone is the music inside of you.
Love reminds me of my best friend.

Lydia Miranda (8)
St Mary's CE (VA) Primary School, Mildenhall

Love

Love tastes like lovely red cherries.
Love smells like wet paint.
Love looks like Miss O'Connell.
Love feels like a hedgehog.
Love reminds me of my mum,
Love sounds like a bunch of girly-girls.
Love is as beautiful as a bunch of roses.
Love is as fantastic as St Mary's School.

Terry Archer (8)
St Mary's CE (VA) Primary School, Mildenhall

Harvest Time

H arvest is a very exciting time of the year
A ll the leaves start to fall, all golden and brown
R ound and brown conkers rolling down the hill, faster and faster
V ibrating leaves against the road
E very day the green grass gets longer and longer
S ee the leaves blowing in the wind
T ractors go along the fields every day.

Ruby Wappett (7)
Tollgate Primary School

Autumn In The Woods

The small, green, glossy moss covered
In a colourful blanket of brown and orange leaves,
Squirrels collecting nuts from large strong oak trees,
Mysterious interesting fungus growing by the bare cold trees.

Lydia Williams (7)
Tollgate Primary School

Apple Limerick

There was an apple that said bye,
He went to bed and woke up in a pie.
I ate him all up,
With tea in a cup,
My belly was so full I thought I might die!

Ryan Gibbs (8)
Tollgate Primary School

Untitled

There once was a pumpkin called Ned
Who liked to sleep in his bed.
One day he fell out
He gave a big shout
And got a big bruise on his head!

Emily Wilding-Smith (8)
Tollgate Primary School

Pumpkin Limerick

There was once a pumpkin that was fat,
It was bright orange and wore a green hat.
It was dirty and round,
And had a shiny crown,
Then got caught by an angry ginger cat.

Katie Hopkins (8)
Tollgate Primary School

Apple Limerick

There was once an apple that was red,
It felt very sleepy so it went to bed.
It was fat, big and round
And it heard a big sound
And that was that, he was dead!

Thomas Dunning (8)
Tollgate Primary School

Carrot Limerick

There was once a carrot called Ray,
He spent all his time eating hay.
When he ran out,
He gave a big shout,
So he starved on his bed all day.

Jordan Rylands-Corcoran (9)
Tollgate Primary School

Rosy The Apple

There once was an apple called Rosy,
Who was sweet and very cosy.
She went to town,
To buy a now gown,
And a bunch of lovely pink posies.

Shannon Wade (8)
Tollgate Primary School

My Silver Bag

In my silver bag I will put . . .
Green slippery moss,
Fluffy clouds and crispy golden leaves.

In my silver bag I will put . . .
Golden, waving, flowing corn,
Shiny, sparkling, grey pebbles and golden, brown, hard conkers.

Finally in my silver bag I will put . . .
Gleaming brown trees,
Red tasty strawberries
And children playing in a leaf pile.

Charlotte Payne (7)
Tollgate Primary School

My Autumn

A spiky brown hedgehog looking for a new warm tree
U nder the trees a pile of leaves
T ime for Hallowe'en
U nder the roof there's a warm red, yellow fire
M others covered in blankets
N ights are black with a white moon.

Harry Barker (7)
Tollgate Primary School

Autumn Days

A way with the leaves, don't get in my way or otherwise
I will squash you
U nder the trees the leaves fall down all gold and brown
T all golden corn all waving in the wind
U sually the floors get mossy and wet
M arrows start to grow on the grassy earth
N arrow roads with leafy grounds.

Jessica Bromley (7)
Tollgate Primary School

Autumn Times

A utumn is a sign of fun
U nder the trees there are lots of leaves
T omorrow I will come back again
U p on the top there are nests in the trees
M orning times the birds lay their eggs
N oon lights up and the hedgehogs roll in.

Ella Jackson (8)
Tollgate Primary School

Autumn Time

A t night it is cold
U nder the trees the leaves look solid and bold
T ime for all the flowers to die
U nder a tree when it is a cold dark night
M y mum says it's autumn again
N ever could I be so happy because it's harvest time again.

Jimi Jameson (8)
Tollgate Primary School

Autumn

A set of crispy leaves
U nder the trees there are leaves
T ime goes quicker
U nder the sky so dark
M others snug in bed
N ight is very dark.

Joshua Rogers-Webb (7)
Tollgate Primary School

Roses

Roses are red
Butterflies are white
Leaves are green
Flowers are yellow
Clouds are blue
Roses are prickly
Leaves are crunchy
Clouds are big
The sun is shiny.

Cheyenne Mitchell (7)
Tollgate Primary School

Animal Poem

Horses like to neigh,
Ponies like to run,
Dogs like to bark,
Animals like to have fun.

Fishes like to swim,
Cats like to purr,
Goats like grass,
Animals have fur.

Amber Gross (7)
Tollgate Primary School

My Teacher

My teacher is the best!
She is called Mrs Wakeman.
Whenever I get in a mess
She says, 'Just start again.'
One day she went off and I said, 'I miss you a lot.'
Then she came back and I said,
'Oh Mrs Wakeman, you are the best one around.'

Eleanor Crowther (7)
Tollgate Primary School

Leaves

Leaves on skates
Just like me
Swirling and waving
Curling and flying
Waving red and yellow.

Lorraine Coleman (7)
Tollgate Primary School

Leaves

Leaves can fly
And can die.
Some are brown.
The leaves fall off.
Leaves are green and crinkly.

Ayesha Fordham (7)
Tollgate Primary School

Autumn

Brown leaves
The moss on the ground
Birds singing
Leaves floating off the trees.

Tommy Bleach (7)
Tollgate Primary School

Autumn

Autumn; the leaves fall off the trees
Brown, yellow and red
The wind blows them about in the air
They end up on the ground.

Connor Fox (7)
Tollgate Primary School

The Lifecycle Of A Leaf

The leaves turn red, they fall to the ground swirling backwards
and forwards.
They land on the ground with no noise at all and then get swept away.
In winter there are no leaves at all,
They've all fallen down, first one by one then two by two.
Then the snow starts to come, white and crunchy.
In summer the leaves turn bright green and are all high up on the trees
But then the leaves turn brown and then go dull like an old time doll.

Max Weston (7)
Tollgate Primary School

Autumn Poem

In autumn the leaves fall down
Red, yellow and golden brown.
They fall to the ground,
There they make a crunchy sound.

Squirrels collect their nuts before winter
Hedgehogs, slugs and bugs
Foxes hide behind the trees
Waiting for their prey.

Michael Hackett & Kloe Childs (7)
Tollgate Primary School

Autumn

In autumn the leaves fall down
Red, yellow and golden brown.
They fall to the ground
Here they make a crunching sound.

Bethany Higgins (7)
Tollgate Primary School

Carrot Limerick

There once was a carrot called Brett,
Who loved heading the ball in the net.
He did a forward roll,
Scored a goal,
It was one the keeper couldn't get.

Callum Dove (9)
Tollgate Primary School

Kate The Onion

There was a young onion called Kate
Whose nose was the size of a plate.
Her legs were so small,
They were no use at all,
But her mouth was as big as a gate.

Matthew Morrissey (8)
Tollgate Primary School

Blackberry Limerick

There once was a blackberry called Ted,
Who always liked staying in bed.
He gave a big shout,
Because he fell out
And landed on top of his head.

Courtney Coleman (9)
Tollgate Primary School

Young Writers Information

We hope you have enjoyed reading this book - and that you will continue to enjoy it in the coming years.

If you like reading and writing poetry drop us a line, or give us a call, and we'll send you a free information pack.

Alternatively if you would like to order further copies of this book or any of our other titles, then please give us a call or log onto our website at www.youngwriters.co.uk

Young Writers Information
Remus House
Coltsfoot Drive
Peterborough
PE2 9JX

(01733) 890066